Attune Your Body
With Dao-In:

Taoist Exercise
For a Long and Happy Life

Masters Series of Taoist Internal Practices

BOOK ONE

Attune Your Body With Dao-In:

Taoist Exercise For a Long and Happy Life

"Revised Edition"

By Hua-Ching Ni

SevenStar Communications
Santa Monica

The College of Tao offers classes on *Dao-In* and other types of movement such as *t'ai chi* and *chi gong*, about health, spirituality and the teachings of the Integral Way by Hua-Ching Ni. To obtain a list of Mentors teaching in your area or country, or to obtain information about the Integral Way of Life Correspondence Course, please write the College of Tao, 1314 Second Street, Santa Monica, CA 90401 USA.

Acknowledgement: Thanks to Suta Cahill, Peter Cunneen, Janet DeCourtney, Frank Gibson, Tiane Sommers and other students in Atlanta for their contribution in editing and preparing this book.

SevenStar Communications Group, Inc.
1314 Second Street
Santa Monica, California 90401

All Rights Reserved. No part of this book may be used or reproduced in any manner whatsoever without written permission, except in the case of brief quotations in articles or reviews.

The paper used in this publication meets the minimum requirements of the American National Standard for Information Sciences Permanence of Paper for Printed Library Materials, ANSI 239.48-1984.

First Edition Copyright 1989, Printed April 1991
Revised Edition Copyright 1994, Printed April 1994

Library of Congress Cataloging-in-Publication Data

Ni, Hua Ching.
    Attune your body with Dao-In : Taoist exercise for a long and happy life / by Hua-Ching Ni. -- Rev. ed.
      p. cm. -- (Masters series of Taoist internal practices : bk. 1)
    Includes index.
    ISBN 0-937064-72-6 : $14.95
    1. Tao yin.   I. Title.   II. Series.
RA781.85.N5   1994   94-12296
613.7'1--dc20   CIP

*This book is dedicated to all who wish to
attain spiritual development
by learning and practicing the physical arts
of the Integral Way.
Your achievement will be greater
by also working on
the internal understanding and practices
suggested in my other books.*

Warning - Disclaimer

This book is intended to present information and techniques that have been in use throughout the Orient for many years. This information and these practices utilize a natural system within the body, however, there are no claims for their effectiveness. The information is offered according to the author's best knowledge and experience and is to be used by the reader at his or her own discretion.

Because of the sophisticated nature of the information contained within this book, it is recommended that before following any of the exercises the reader(s) should first consult his or her physician on whether or not the reader(s) should embark on the physical activity described herein. The author and publisher of this book are not responsible for any injury which may occur through following the instructions in this book.

It is recommended that the reader of this book also study the author's other books for further knowledge about a healthy lifestyle and energy conducting exercises.

To female readers,

According to the teaching of the Integral Way, male and female are equally important in the natural sphere. This is illustrated in the diagram of *T'ai Chi*. Thus, discrimination is not practiced in our tradition. All of my work is dedicated to both genders of humanity.

Wherever possible, constructions using masculine pronouns to represent both sexes are avoided; where they do occur, we ask your tolerance and spiritual understanding. We hope that you will take the essence of my teaching and overlook the superficiality of language. Gender discrimination is inherent in English; ancient Chinese pronouns do not have differences of gender. I wish that all of you will achieve yourselves above the level of language and gender.

Thank you, H. C. Ni

Contents

List of Exercises *i*

Prelude *iii*

Preface *iv*

1. What is Dao-In? 1
2. Dao-In for Self-Cultivation 7
3. Dao-In for Self-Management 15
4. Important Guidelines for Practicing Dao-In 22
5. Dao-In: The Integral Way of Conducting Energy in the Body 30

        Preliminary Section 30
        Main Section 57
        Concluding Section 107
        Optional Section 114

Afterword 117

List of Exercises

PRELIMINARY SECTION - PART I
1. The Immortal Awakening from Napping 30
2. Immortal Straightening the Leg 31
3. Immortal Imitating Butterfly Opening Its Wings 33
4. Immortal Tightening the Body Like a Bow 36
5. Immortal Imitating Grazing Horse Raising Its Head 37
6. Immortal Embracing the Universe 37
7. Immortal Lifting the Mountain 38

PRELIMINARY SECTION - PART II
8. The Immortal Imitating the Owl Turning Its Head 41
9. Immortal Imitating Bamboo Bending in the Wind 42
10. Immortal Imitating a Sea Lion Raising Its Head 44
11. Immortal Imitating a Blue Jay Looking Behind Him 45

PRELIMINARY SECTION - PART III
12. Immortal Imitating the Lazy Tiger Stretching 47
13. Immortal Imitating Peacock Turning and Looking at Tail Feathers 51
14. The Immortal Stretching Well 53
15. Immortal Pulling Bow String 54

MAIN SECTION - PART I
16. Immortal Imitating a Tall Pine Standing Firmly in the Wind 57
17. Immortal Imitating a Lizard Turning to Watch a Dragonfly 58
18. Immortal Massaging the Wind Pond Point 60
19. Immortal Beating the Heavenly Drum 60
20. Immortal Sounding the Heavenly Bell 61
21. Immortal Pressing the Sun and Moon Corners 62
22. Immortal Turning to Look Back 62
23. Immortal Imitating a Bird Turning Its Head 63
24. Immortal Shaking the Immortal Peach Tree 64

MAIN SECTION - PART II
25. Immortal Imitating a Bird Washing Its Wings 66
26. Dragon Stretching Its Paws 67
27. Immortal Stretching the Bow 68
28. Immortal Holding Up the Sky 69
29. Immortal Fortifying the Great Wall 70
30. Immortal Turning to Look at the Moon 72
31. Red Dragon Stirring the Sea 73
32. Slowly Turning the Earth 74

MAIN SECTION - PART III
33. Immortal Turning the Pulley to Raise the Energy 75
34. Immortal Imitating a Hummingbird's Flight 75
35. Dragon Dance 76
36. Immortal Imitating the Descending Stars 78
37. Immortal Imitating Wind Dispersing the Clouds 79
38. Immortal Strengthening the Pillars 38
39. Immortal Watching Twin Flying Horses Scratching Each Other 81
40. Immortal Beating the Round Drum 83
41. Immortal Opening the Heavenly Gate 84

MAIN SECTION - PART IV

42. Immortal Imitating the Wriggle of the Young Dragon 85
43. The Immortal's Delight 86
44. Immortal Holding the Foot to Strengthen the Knee 88
45. Immortal Bowing to the Rising Sun 89
46. Immortal Pressing Kun Lun Mountain 90
47. Immortal Stimulating the Scalp 92
48. Immortal Turning the Gristwheel 92
49. Immortal in Sitting Meditation 93

MEDITATION POSTURES

1. Divine One of Wholeness 95
2. Divine One of Subtle Integration 96
3. Divine One of Peaceful-Mindedness 97
4. Divine One of Perfect Harmony 97
5. Divine One of Equal Mindedness 97
6. Divine One of Constant Subtle Virtue 98
7. Divine One of Original Simplicity 98
8. Divine One of Trustworthiness 99
9. Divine One of Universal Mastery 99
10. Divine One of Undefeatable Plainness 99
11. Divine One of Non-Aggression 100
12. Divine One of Unconditional Supportiveness 101
13. Divine One of Pervasive Harmony 101
14. Divine One of Subtle Universal Law 101
15. Divine One of Subtle Light 102
16. Divine One of Total Integration 102
17. Divine One of Life-Giving Vitalization 103
18. Divine One of Unaffected Clarity 103
19. Divine One of Great Silent Eloquence 104
20. Divine One of Highest Awareness 105
21. Divine One of Honest Nature 105

CONCLUDING SECTION

50. Immortal Warming Up the Eyes 107
51. Immortal Practicing Temple Acupressure 108
52. Immortal Massaging the Nose 108
53. Immortal Doing Eye Acupressure 109
54. Immortal Relaxing Neck Muscles 110
55. Immortal Sharpening the Hearing 110
56. Immortal Experiencing Gentle Rainfall 111
57. Immortal Imitating a Woodpecker 112
58. Immortal Letting Go 112
59. Lying Meditation 113

OPTIONAL SECTION

60. Immortal Strengthening His Abdomen 114
61. Immortal Guarding His Energy 114
62. Immortal's Breath Taming Active Energy 115
63. Immortal Strengthening Vital Energy 115
64. Immortal Strengthening Self 115

Prelude

The Subtle Essence conveyed by the teaching of the Integral Way is the deep truth of all religions, yet it transcends all religions, leaving them behind like clothing worn in different seasons or places. The teaching of the Subtle Essence includes everything of religious importance, yet it goes beyond the level of religion. It directly serves your life, surpassing the boundary of all religions and extracting the essence of them all.

The Subtle Essence as conveyed by the teaching of the Integral Way is also the goal of all sciences, but it surpasses all sciences, leaving them behind as partial and temporal descriptions of this universal Integral Truth. Unlike any partial science, the Way goes beyond the level of any single scientific search.

The Subtle Essence is the master teaching. It does not rely on any authority. It is like a master key which can unlock all doors directly leading you to the inner room of the ultimate truth. It is not frozen at the emotional surface of life. It does not remain locked at the level of thought or belief with the struggling which extends to skepticism and endless searching.

The teaching of the One Great Path of the Subtle Essence presents the core of the Integral Truth and helps you reach it yourself.

Preface

In 1989, with the publication of the Story of Two Kingdoms, I knew I had come to a stage where I needed to teach different practices that could guide those who truly wished to achieved themselves spiritually by realizing what I describe in my books. In 1990 I put my lectures, made during my 1989 travels, into about ten books for students and readers who are now moving to a deeper stage. This is a time of new enlightenment for people who are working deeply within themselves and in the external world.

I now offer the teaching of physical movement for spiritual learning through videotapes and books of *t'ai chi* movement and *dao-in* practices. My physical strength to accomplish this task is invigorated by the movements presented in these publications. I hope you can use the ones that suit you and that they will contribute to your positive and virtuous life.

Your spiritual friend,

Ni, Hua-Ching
September 1, 1990
In the Mountains of Southern Oregon

Chapter 1

What is *Dao-In*?

Dao-In is the Chinese word for physical energy conducting. As a set of rhythmic movements, it adjusts and attunes as it generates and strengthens one's personal energy. This book presents a series of traditional *Dao-In* exercises.

Ancient people were much less complex than people are today. There were wise people among them, but they were not idealistic, nor were they emotionally motivated to fill the emptiness of their lives. Rather than indulging in religious fantasies or in abstract knowledge for its own sake, they preferred something practical that could help their lives.

Living conditions today are very different from those of even a few hundred years ago; you can imagine how differently people must have lived ten thousand years ago. People in the wilderness sat, but had no chair. They ate, but had no table. There were no rugs on the floor, and the unavoidable result of sitting on the floor was arthritis or rheumatism in the joints and bones, even for healthy people. These conditions are the result of stagnation, which happens when physical energy does not move inside the body.

Wise people tried to find a practical way to break up the stagnation of physical energy, and this is how different methods of physical energy conductance developed among people in the region of the Yellow River in China. Once they began doing physical energy conducting, they discovered that not only did it solve the problem of energy stagnation, but it also improved their general health and lengthened their lives.

The people who lived by the Yellow River became ambitious and used these same practices to fulfill their desire to live even longer. They understood the limitations of the body, but they eventually learned how to combine or utilize natural energy to sustain their natural life, resulting in longevity and sometimes spiritual immortality.

Dao-In has become part of the immortal cultivation of the Integral Way of Life that was developed by many generations of spiritually achieved people. It is also a part of Traditional Chinese Medicine which not only prescribes herbs but also recommends certain movements as ways to recover from problems such as physical energy imbalance and illness.

Movement, or exercise, is one part of holistic or integral medicine. It is also a form of self-cultivation, because it makes you vigorous and energetic. It generates energy and helps you break up emotional problems. A long list of aspects of a person's negative temperament will no longer apply to the person who does these exercises and reforms his or her personal energy (see Chapter 2). These exercises will make your energy tick and make you feel truly happy emotionally. They are not passive spiritual practices that will sedate you; rather, they will constantly enliven you.

Dao-In is suitable for people of all ages. If you have time, you can do the whole set of movements. If you are interested in only certain sections or have a limited amount of time, then you can do just a few sections. It is completely flexible and individual.

For a serious student of longevity and spiritual immortality, the foundation is here. Although deep understanding is important, actual practice is the most essential thing. If you truly wish to practice spiritual self-cultivation and you attain good understanding without ever realizing your goals through regular practice, you will not achieve the desired result. Only when you do these exercises with deep understanding will they be beneficial.

For those who are seeking physical improvement, *Dao-In* will definitely help you. In your daily life, you cannot avoid doing a little heavy work sometimes. Also, if you are married, there is an obligation; occasionally you must have sex and so forth. You must have and use those energies to live in the world. One purpose of *Dao-In* is to make you fit to accomplish what you need to do in your life. It is not a self-centered, limiting exercise or meditation that makes you weak, unfit or unsuited for helping others.

With this understanding, you can practice *Dao-In* naturally, with positive results that can come faster than you might expect. Sometimes we call these results "immortal medicine," because you can feel a change almost immediately. It is because these valuable exercises work so well that they have been maintained for so many generations in our tradition. In the last generation, nobody taught them. People saw pictures in ancient books, but nobody really learned them. So their high value was not fully revealed to the general public until now.

If you learn from a good teacher, you will see how simple it is. It is not a tedious intellectual process. As you do it, you produce good and fast results.

Over a long period of time and through many generations, the tradition of the Integral Way has slowly filtered out ineffective practices and kept those which are useful. *Dao-In* (pronounced dow-een), as a form of energy conductance, is sometimes compared to *hatha yoga*. The theory of *hatha yoga* is very close to that of *Dao-In* which is based on the principle of *yin* and *yang*. The pure purpose of *Dao-In* is spiritual self-cultivation. It benefits the individual who practices it.

The origin of many *Dao-In* exercises is the *Taoist Canon*, a large collection of ancient spiritual books compiled in China around 1436 to 1449 A.D. Many of these movements are very ancient. They are mostly for healing or increasing one's health. In ancient times, *Dao-In* was not taught to the public; it was taught to some special individuals for personal attunement, adjustment, refreshment or amusement. No one, therefore, in recent history has had sufficient practical experience or training to really know how to do these movements. They have only created more and more flowery postures, but the effect was not the same as what you find here, which originated directly from ancient spiritual development. The achievements or discoveries that were passed down for tens of thousands of years have come to be known culturally as "Taoism." The ancient achieved ones who knew something about basic physical energy conducting stood out as examples of high spiritual achievement and were greatly admired by people. Some were more highly achieved than others, and those highly achieved ones who were recognized as immortals inspired confidence in the effectiveness of the practices they did.

Dao-In is more than an art; it also has a spiritual goal. It was originally a complete school of life containing the original practices of the immortal tradition of the Integral Way. This is what I teach.

Internal energy conductance is closely connected with Traditional Chinese Medicine in its focus on the physical aspects of the body. I will offer a few sentences from the teaching of Lao Tzu to illustrate the purpose of these exercises. I hope these excerpts will help you understand the benefit of adopting such a practice in your life.

In the third chapter of the *Tao Teh Ching*, Lao Tzu states:

*The developed one keeps his mind unoccupied
    and his energy substantially within.
He weakens his ambition,
    and strengthens his bone.*

Now, how do you strengthen your bone? The answer lies within the exercises and by physical energy conductance.

A strong bone is supported by fresh marrow. People keep themselves young or rejuvenate themselves by doing good exercises that affect the health of the bones with sufficient and young marrow.

In Chapter 76 of the *Tao Teh Ching*, Lao Tzu says,

*When people are alive,
    their bodies are soft and supple.
When people die,
    they are stiff and hardened.*

When trees, grass and animals are alive,
  they are soft and pliable.
When they are dead,
  they become dry and brittle.

From Lao Tzu's words, we know that to be hard and stiff is to be a student of death. To maintain softness and suppleness is to be a student of life. Now, let us look at Chapter 78, in which Lao Tzu says,

Under heaven there is nothing more flexible
  than water.
However, anything stronger than water
  cannot beat the water.
Therefore, it is true that the soft
  and gentle can overcome the strong.

I think this is enough to give a picture of why it is important to do *Dao-In*. Lao Tzu himself did *Dao-In*. Some say he lived to be 260 years old.

All the achieved ones of the Integral Way spoke or wrote about the subtle energy that cannot be described. Whether it is named or unnamed, this energy cannot be put into words. Nevertheless, I like to describe this subtle power or energy as "universal vitality." That is a useful name for it: universal vitality.

How can we maintain the vitality which we receive from the universe? There is a practice, a method, a way of life in which one learns to be soft and gentle, not only mentally, but physically as well. It is what I call the Integral Way.

Pong Tzu was another spiritually achieved one who lived earlier and to a much older age than Lao Tzu. Legend says that Pong Tzu lived to be 800 years old. He truly knew how to eat, how to conduct his energy and how to have sex without harming his life. Many good types of knowledge were contained in this one person. They are all profound treasures of great spiritual value.

Spiritual immortality is based on the truth that energy is transformable. The process of sublimation takes energy of a low level and transforms it to a point where it is no longer scattered. Sublimation unifies all that we have been given by nature.

Nature equips us with five senses which enable us to know the world around us: the eyes see, the ears hear, the nostrils smell, the tongue tastes and body feels. Once you are disarmed of all senses, for natural or unnatural reasons, then your spirit may learn to ride something else such as an animal or another human being, but if you do so, then you take on the trouble of that form of life.

Through the gradual process of spiritual self-cultivation, the coarse energy of the body is transformed into spiritual energy. After the physical foundation of life is dissolved, the spirit exists independently of the senses, yet you have keen, direct intuition and powers of perception.

Many people force themselves to sit and concentrate or discipline themselves to recite mantras and prayers. Those practices are ineffective, because there is still a kind of scatteredness, and such practices are usually psychological approaches. They are different from practices that have been developed through observance of subtle spiritual law. Not until you learn internal transformation, sublimation, and reintegration will the effort of such concentration and recitations bring any result other than making you feel better for a short while.

In Los Angeles, my sons promote and teach a series of movements called the Eight Treasures, or *Pa Kun Dao-In*, which are the energy conducting exercises of eight masters who lived at the beginning of the Han Dynasty. They are usually practiced outdoors in a standing position. In this book, I am introducing a collection of exercises from all the great masters of the Integral Way who practiced *Dao-In* indoors on a mat. I offer these movements as a solid foundation to those who are interested in doing meditation and spiritual self-cultivation and who wish a good result beyond physical forms.

Chapter 2

Dao-In for Self-Cultivation

Dao-In is adaptable to many situations and is easy to learn. It benefits your health and is especially helpful for people who have concentrated on intellectual pursuits for many years.

There are five basic parts to the whole system of *Dao-In*. Three parts comprise the physical foundation, which supports your health and can make you generally stronger. In one part, there is a special healing purpose for each movement, which refreshes, attunes and invigorates your energy. For example, if someone sits too long in meditation because they wish to see a special result, they produce a kind of acid in the body by remaining motionless. *Dao-In* can rectify that.

It is important to understand the physical management of your own body when you do *Dao-In* and in daily life as well. The mind always needs to take executive responsibility in all situations. A special section teaches you about physical management. Another is for meditation.

Many people believe that meditation can bring about spiritual achievement. However, one's spirit can also be nurtured within the body through proper sitting, standing, lying and moving. All good body positions still need some adjustment, especially if you stay in one position too long because of office work, meditation or illness perhaps. *Dao-In* essentially refreshes, attunes, adjusts and regenerates personal energy, providing a healthy balance for people who sit a lot or are physically inactive.

Dao-In contains a wide variety of movements from many systems. It is a heritage from the integral beings known as immortals and was passed down in this long tradition known as the Integral Way. It has been proven over time to aid personal health.

Dao-In was developed to relieve physical energy stagnation. For example, if you lie down too long, when you get up you will be stiff, or part of your body will be sore. If you walk too long, stand too long, sit too long or do physical work too long, some muscles, or the muscles of the entire body, will react. This includes tendons, and even cartilage and bones. The principle behind doing *Dao-In* is to make timely adjustments to your physical energy. When you get up and practice a few movements, then the energy flow inside also changes. You can learn to conduct or return the energy flow in your body to a condition of normalcy. If, when you first feel signs of stagnation, you immediately move, the stagnation will go away and the energy will return to a more balanced and proper flow. Many physical problems are caused by an imbalance of internal and external yin and yang. They can also be caused by a nervous system, circulatory system or other system that is too strong; the other systems are weak in contrast, so there is imbalance. Energy conductance, or *Dao-In*, can help you balance yourself, internally and externally. Externally, it helps muscles, tendons and bones. Internally, it helps the different systems of the body, including circulation, secretion and so forth to function better.

You can do *Dao-In* on any occasion when you feel the need by rubbing your neck and face, etc. You do not need to wait until you have a whole block of time to lie down and exercise. The practical application of *Dao-In* during daily life is to use it when you feel the need to move your arms, stretch your spine, rub your feet, or other similar adjustments.

In many situations, you can respond naturally to a bodily need. Ignoring a signal from the body can cause trouble. This is true of any kind of body signal and is not just related to staying in one position for a long time. For example, if you eat food that causes a bad reaction, and you continue to eat that food, it will cause trouble for you sooner or later. Small things that seem shallow and unimportant are not trivial. Knowing what to do and when to make a change depends on nurturing your spiritual sensitivity. You must respond to your environment and to your physical foundation. If a signal or message about a developing problem reaches the brain and you immediately address it, then trouble will not result.

Everything affects your practice and gives it a different effect. *Dao-In* does not need to be done in a standard way, like a schoolbook exercise for the sake of discipline. It is totally different, because it is a pure reaction to an internal need. Keep in mind that your results will depend on how you do it: how well you learn it, how much you do it, and whether you do it vigorously or gently.

The Concluding Section of *Dao-In* is focused primarily work on the face and head. This can easily be done when you are sitting in an office, traveling on an airplane or meeting with people. The Concluding Section is especially helpful after meditation or after sitting too long in any situation.

The whole set of movements can be done as a daily routine when you have the time. You can also alternate it with other exercises like *t'ai chi*. You do not need to do all the exercises from beginning to end, one by one, all the time. When you feel the need, pick up one and adjust yourself. In that way, *Dao-In* can be really helpful in your everyday life. It is definitely a trustworthy and valuable friend that is suitable for all ages.

Every day is the foundation of your long, happy life. Modern people do not have much time to take care of themselves, but your life is still yours, so you should learn to take care of yourself. Learning to do so is not hard, and the knowledge is useful. It does not conflict with your spiritual, political or intellectual background. None of those things are related deeply to your life. Thus, *Dao-In* is something that can be used universally by all people. It was used in ancient times, is used in modern times and will be used in the future, unless in the future people no longer have a physical form. Perhaps they will live in the air or have an ethereal body that is different from the physical body. In that case, there will be no problem of energy stagnation!

When you do *Dao-In*, the most important thing is relaxation. As you are lying down, feel as though you have been in a cave for a thousand years. You are totally relaxed. You are a spirit who has come to earth from the sky, and you have just woken up in a human body. The first thing you are aware of is the sense of breathing. From gentle breathing, slowly flex your muscles by making all kinds of movements. By the principle of increasing gradually, you add a little strength, and then some more, in stages. Do not do anything too suddenly, but make progress bit by bit. Then you will become strong. When you do these exercises, your breathing should be naturally deep.

Chuang Tzu described a "true human" in his writings. He talked about ancient times when there were many different animals on earth. Some humans originated from certain animals, however, the source of "true humans" is Heaven or the stars. "True humans" have certain purely spiritual functions, not only high physical-spiritual functions.

When, as a true human, you wake up, the Earth spirit and the Heaven spirit are integrated, and you wake up as a flesh and blood life. In this cave, there is no mother to nurse you with milk, but there is nutrition in the air and the surrounding energy. So you ingest air and energy. You start to move. Your movements are not just movements; all movements help you take in the natural nutrition around you. Air is a kind of flowing energy like water, but you do not see it. So you drink the air and the more subtle surrounding energy.

The key to doing *Dao-In* lies two main guidelines. One guideline is to open each cell to the fresh air. (Chuang Tzu says that the breath should reach the heels.) In doing this exercise, I encourage you to breathe deeply, drawing fresh energy into each cell of the body. This will not only improve your health, but your personality as well.

The second guideline is to use all the postures and movements to unite yourself with the natural environment.

They can restore you to being like a new baby of a heavenly father and earthly mother.

In the *Tao Teh Ching*, there is a description of baby-like spiritual wholeness. All the movements of *Dao-In* exercise help restore a baby-like or soft condition. When you do them, it does not matter how much time you have or how many movements you do at one sitting. Do not rush the movements to fit them into a limited time, but take as much time as each movement requires. Even if you do only a few, do them well. The length of time you practice is less important than practicing each movement slowly and well, keeping your attention on what you are doing. Doing something thoroughly is called "finding immortality in every second of your life." This is the true meaning of immortality.

During the meditative part of *Dao-In*, you sit quietly. Whatever length of time you spend doing the movement part of *Dao-In*, an equal amount of time should be spent sitting in meditative stillness. For example, if you do a half hour of *Dao-In* movement, the sitting meditation should also be a half hour, more or less.

Meditation has different purposes with different postures and different functions. Most of the postures can be classified into one of three categories. If the posture focuses on the upper part of the body, it moves the energy higher. If the hand posture is a little lower, it maintains the energy lower. If the exercise is focused in the middle of the body, it usually gathers the energy to be centered there.

The purpose of the postures in meditation is to nurture your energy. This is beneficial. The postures came from the ancient culture of about a million years ago when people first discovered that different postures had different effects on life and on internal development. For a long time, the knowledge of these postures was scattered, but it was eventually gathered into one place and presented as a whole teaching and training, an entire school of *Dao-In*.

Select the meditation postures that you feel are suited to your need at a particular time. Learn and practice them according to your own experience. There may be one or several postures which suit you, either in one session or during one period of your life. It is wise to choose one, experience it deeply, and benefit from it, instead of doing them all with less result.

These postures are for the pure purpose of nurturing or attuning your internal energy. For example, for young people it is hard to maintain internal peace. Because their sexual energy and impulses are too strong, it makes them imbalanced so that they follow external attractions too easily. Therefore, if you are young and strong, your hand posture needs to be higher. Older people's energy is weak in the lower area, so a good meditation posture for them starts from the lower center and moves to the middle center.

Some centered postures are suitable for different occasions and purposes. If you do *Dao-In* or quiet sitting to nurture your *chi,* be sure that you do not carry any disturbing emotion into your practice. Emotion will deform your internal energy. It brings no benefit, and may cause serious damage. Generally speaking, if you can manage your emotion and practice quiet meditation in your life, it will always have a positive effect.

A troubled mind can be helped by working on the body, and *Dao-In* promotes good mental health as well as emotional balance.

Religious teachers attempt to use the mind to help itself, but this usually creates psychological traps. Nature equips us sufficiently to be able to help ourselves, but a person must guard oneself from negative energy in order to maintain a natural, healthy life. The ancient achieved ones who did that for themselves developed good ways to help others break through all their self-created obstacles, and *Dao-In* is among them.

Negative energy can manifest as:

bitterness
dissatisfaction in life achievement

unformed life goal
lack of persistence toward the goal of life
aloofness
pride
lack of protection against outside negative influence
craving for power
ruthlessness
domineering personality
overly strenuous
physical trauma
indecisiveness
inflexibility
rigidity
fearfulness
self-blame
exhaustion
purposeless struggling
negligence in serious duty
gloominess
inferior behavior
impotence
hatefulness
jealousy
self-obsession
despair
discouragement
inadequate personal growth
aggressiveness (inconsiderate action)
self-pity
excessive confidence
repeating big mistakes
resentment
bad temper
lack of confidence
weak will
arrogance
criticism
anxiety
inner torture by conflict of emotion and motivation

14 Attune Your Body with Dao-In

The practice of *Dao-In* can help you overcome negative energy and assist your spirit in becoming as sweet and fragrant as a rose.

Chapter 3

Dao-In for Self-Management

The purpose of *Dao-In* is good management of the body. The ancient developed ones who followed the Integral Way of life believed that managing the body was like managing the government of a country. The body is a country or a society, and the mind is the executive or president. The wise executive (mind) of a healthy country (body) considers itself an employee or public servant of the country, not its ruler. Some ancient kings or leaders were tyrants rather than effective rulers. A tyrant (a misapplied mind) ignores the signals of trouble and is self-indulgent, thus bringing disaster to the country (body).

When we do *Dao-In* or any spiritual practice, it helps us learn how to manage life better. Life is internal and external. Internal is what you cannot see. I use the external to help you understand the internal. We talk about the environment as something external; it is a part of our life's management. We need a good, healthy environment.

In ancient times, a person could avoid social and political interference by hiding in the mountains where nobody could reach them. Today, things have changed. No one can afford to ignore the political environment.

Chinese people suffered from the evil force that had its root, not in China, but in the negative aspect of human nature called jealousy.

Communism has existed in some Chinese families for thousands of years. If a farmer owns a piece of land and has three children, they all need to work together on the land. It does not matter who is smarter or more diligent, they are treated almost exactly the same, and their rights are equal. Central control naturally rests with the parents, usually with just the father or the mother. That kind of family does not usually do well or prosper, and the emotion of jealousy grows in such an environment.

There is another type of farming family. This family has three or four children, but because they do not have land, they do not have anything, so each of the sons needs to find his own way to grow and prosper, and bring something back to serve the family. This type of family usually does much better than the family that is under central control. They might be jealous initially, but that jealousy changes to become the force of self-improvement.

Anything managed by a government is extreme because of the centralization of authority. Likewise, if you try to extend the mind's absolute control, you will fail because your body functions according to nature. It is the ambition of the mind that tries to organize everything in the individual's life. The mind does not see the reality and consider the other partners involved. If the body feels thirsty, it needs to drink water. Good water is enough, but the mind looks for something like beer or soft drinks or wine. That is called central control.

Let us say the person drinks a lot of cold beer. Then, the mind will say, "Let's go to sleep," and the person sleeps. The sleeping mind does not listen to the body which says, "We need to get up and urinate to get rid of the waste water." Central control has decided, so the body becomes sluggish. What happens in the long term? Urine is a kind of poison; if it accumulates, the body contains a lot of waste water and trouble begins to appear.

Generally speaking, the purpose of a government is to serve the people, just as the purpose of a mind is to serve the life. The opposite is to make the life serve the mind and make the people serve the government; you can see this in countries such as China. The mind is the government and the body is the people. The mind should serve the life: the whole country, all the people. The mind should not indulge in unrestrained fun or in struggles over hegemony in society and the world.

The Integral Way represents a balanced life. If your mind and body get a break from their overly extended desires and dominant daily activities, they can devote some time to your life itself. Then your spiritual energy will grow, be more active and more serviceable. If you rush around, interested only in the mind or body, then you will have no time to nurture your spirit.

What most people do is learn to develop their mind which then serves the lower sphere of life: desire. The mind does not know which desire is right and which is wrong, which is beneficial or unbeneficial to the entirety of one's life. It simply follows desires without considering whether its ends have been obtained by righteous means. People demand a better government, but they never think about their own personal government. Their life is still in an undeveloped condition with a poor government.

In general life, most behavior comes either from the mind commanding the body or the body commanding the mind. Their interplay fulfills the basic necessities of natural life. When social considerations are involved, behavior can become partial and upset the balance between the mind and the body. Partiality can cause trouble for oneself or others who participate in a similar project.

In practicing *Dao-In*, the highest principle is for the developed mind to guide and assist the body in spontaneous movement for self-attunement. *Dao-In* is not a single command from one source; it is a process entailing great cooperation and integration.

Desire does not serve the entire body. Desire is usually an expression of one part of the body or mind and it leaves no room for growth of the spirit. The world's troubles, in large part, are the result of some one overextending his or her desires.

The centralization of all authority represents the desire or ambition of the mind which is blind to the existence of natural function. The living organism of a society and the individual should be served and protected. Leaders like Hitler or Stalin or Mao Tse Tung are examples of bad life management produced by the mind.

Masculine energy, more or less, likes to be in control of a situation. The wise ones are more open, and the stupid ones like more control. Mao Tse Tung brought disaster to China. His students and comrades have only one dream:

"Now it is my turn to enjoy the taste of central control and sit on the throne." So a ghost sits on the Chinese throne and government officials cook the people, stew the people, and use the people for their enjoyment, but they are stupid cooks who kill hens to take eggs. They were never correctly trained. The ruler of a country, according to ancient custom, is like a cook. A cook who is interested only in personal desire, personal interest or personal style without considering the interests of the people, cannot serve their needs.

Two thousand five hundred years ago, early sages like Wen Tzu (a disciple of Lao Tzu) emphasized one word: law. They came to know that only a good system would establish an orderly society that would not serve one individual's self-interest. China has law, but they are tyrannically decided laws that serve the leaders, not the people. In personal life management, enjoyment has limitations. For example, rich and tasty food is not enjoyable if you overeat and have indigestion. To enjoy good things is the ambition or desire of the mind, not the body. When that occurs, there is no internal harmony.

Unless you are highly talented, have righteous virtue or truly understand that you were born to serve your generation, do not seek leadership. If you are born to accomplish something, then the natural opportunity will come to you to do it. Evil competition manifests in killing, harming or suppressing others and only engenders immoral leaders who do a worse job than the ones before them. Seizing power is a desire of the mind. Anything that comes from desire is not balanced.

Do not let any emotional or physical desires overextend themselves to harm the substance of your life. If you do, you will lose the opportunity for spiritual growth. Too many people die without developing their personal spirits, and their lives are wasted.

I would like to share a deep spiritual secret with you. The Japanese invaded China and killed many people during the Sino-Japanese war. All those who were killed by the

Japanese were reborn in Japan and now enjoy whatever that society needed to give to them. The Japanese who were killed, lost their souls in China and could not return to Japan; they were reborn as Chinese idiots or mental inferiors because part of their soul was missing.

As another example, European settlers killed many Native Americans in the United States. Those who were killed have been reborn into Caucasian families to enjoy and inherit the land. Natural balance and natural retribution is subtle but sure. Retribution also happens at the end of the life of an individual who has seized something wrongly. Through spiritual development, you understand that you really wish to take nothing from people, because you need to return what you have taken.

According to old-fashioned religious teachings, retribution is carried out by God. In natural spiritual truth, it is a personal spiritual process. If you have learned the law of energy response, you know that the type of energy frequency you have attracts the same type of energy to yourself. This is not caused only by personal behavior; it can be caused by a habitual pattern of thoughts. Evil begets evil and good begets good. This is truthful knowledge which accurately describes one's personal spiritual energy projection. You do not need to wait for an external spiritual authority to judge, punish and reward you. You are the one who accumulates good and bad things around you as the content of your life.

Reincarnation of a soul into a new life defies all limitations of race, family or tribe. Understanding this spiritual fact will help you know that narrow racial and nationalistic views are short-lived and have no profound spiritual meaning. Spiritual integration by souls reborn to different places, families and races has been happening globally since humans began warring with one another in the world. The blending will continue to move in the direction of spiritual oneness, just as their blood is blended by interbreeding and inter-marriage.

Although conventional religious teaching is inaccurate, the spiritual truth of the result is the same. Thus, you do not need to fear God, you need to fear what you do, say and think.

During the last part of his life, Mao Tse Tung was partially possessed. His soul was halfway suppressed by other strong souls coming in, who said, "Okay, you enjoyed the throne, let us share it too." There is a spiritual practice in China which results from the spiritual chaos of people who have no spiritual discipline. A strong soul can enter another person's body to enjoy their false achievement obtained by improper means. A position and its enjoyment, if not obtained by righteousness, creates an opening for stronger souls to enter and take over for their own enjoyment. They become boss, and the person's fame and life are defeated. The person's own soul is locked up in the lower Tan Tien without any chance to go up to the head, the personal throne. My advice is to sit well on your throne of life and do your job. You have no need to be ambitious for the false throne of the world, unless you are born a natural sun energy of a bright future for the human world.

In China's history, many emperors eliminated their enemies on the way to the throne, but all the enemies who were killed came back to the emperors' families and became their descendants. Thus, the dead enemies returned to the world, enjoyed the throne and caused the emperors to fail miserably before suffering in the shadow world. Only spiritual development can see those things. This is why it is better to live a moderate life and practice fairness, justness and righteousness, without overextending your personal desire or taking anything you do not deserve or that belongs to others. This knowledge can be useful for you in setting up your own government of your individual life.

If you open your eyes widely, you will see that there are only a few developed nations that respect individual human rights. The leaders of many countries are no better than those of modern China. China has a big population and a long history of cultural achievement. It should make the best model of a good and spiritually developed country. Why then do Chinese leaders learn from bad examples? I think it is easy to learn how to follow your desires, but the personal and the social cost is high.

I was born in China and have deep affection for it. I hope my words and comments here become only a historical footnote to a new China. In the tradition of the Integral Way, we focus on individual life. When we talk about a country, it is a metaphor for our body and life.

Dao-In offers adjustment so that you may properly manage your body and govern your life. Through relaxation, attunement and regeneration, you are refreshed and can unite with the natural environment. With each movement, you enjoy the natural nutrition of the air and surrounding energy. From this position, you can develop wholly by maintaining the balance between your body, mind and spirit.

Chapter 4

Important Guidance for Practicing *Dao-In*

I recommend *Dao-In* as a regular practice for those who have the interest. It is suitable to do *Dao-In* during the morning or before 4 or 5 o'clock in the afternoon. If you practice it too late in the day, you will invigorate your energy and will need to calm it down in order to sleep peacefully. The natural way of life is to be active in the morning and early afternoon. It is not wise to be active at high noon or in the evening.

The other time that is good for exercise is after midnight. At midnight, the earth turns toward the rising sun. The diagram of *T'ai Chi* ☯ illustrates this understanding of the day's energy. One side of the diagram is mostly white and the other is mostly black. The midline represents both midnight (the start of early morning) and noon (when the solar energy begins to retreat). The best energy time for assisting human health, according to ancient knowledge, is from midnight to noon, but noon itself is not suitable for activity because the energy is too coarse or strong at that time.

If you choose *Dao-In* as your main exercise, practice, or cultivation, I suggest that you eat less, and that you eat foods that are light and soft. If you eat too much or you eat foods that are too solid and heavy, your body will be preoccupied with digestion and exercise will only disturb the natural digestive process. Some people eat four meals a day, and some even eat all day long. When you do that, your body has no time to work on anything but digestion. You should also go to sleep early, if possible. If you go to sleep late and get up late, then you lose the golden energy hours of each day.

In modern life, personal leisure activities are usually done in the evening. This is suitable for social activities or attending a class. *Dao-In* is best taught and learned in the day time; however, because of modern work schedules, it is all right to learn it in the evening. Just do not practice it at night.

You might try doing the whole set of *Dao-In* exercises in the evening, avoiding movements that stimulate the head. If you can still sleep well, I think it would be okay, because *Dao-In* not only wakes you up, it can also make you sleep soundly. It all depends on which postures or movements you do. If you learn the form in the evening, do it gently. The best hours for practice are in the morning.

Dao-In can be practiced indoors or outdoors. A meadow is good. Whether you do it outside or inside, choose a quiet place that is not dusty. Spread a thick blanket or mat over the ground or floor. If it is indoors, open the windows or use an electric fan to blow out the bad energy before you begin.[1] (Make sure to turn the fan off when you begin the exercise.) If you practice in your room, some indoor plants or fresh flowers are suitable to have around, but not cactus. Cactus does not help your energy.

Perhaps you would rather take a blanket and do your exercise under the trees or in a meadow. It is always okay to do it indoors on a rainy day; just open the window or adjust the condition inside of the room before you begin.

Do not have any pets around while you exercise. Pets have their own energy and odor; do not confuse it with your own. When you do *Dao-In*, be clean, beneficial and supportive to yourself.

If you have a cold or if you are tired or overexcited, restore your health before you do *Dao-In*. *Dao-In* is more beneficial if you are in a normal and relaxed situation.

The benefit of any system of exercise, especially energy conducting exercise, depends on how much time and concern you have for your body. *Dao-In* is a good, effective

---

[1] You can refresh and change the air inside your house each day. Modern houses do not have many windows. If the house is big and deep, it may have stagnant energy. The floor plan and design determines the energy flow of the house.

system of bodily movement. You will definitely be rewarded if you invest the time and energy to do it.

It is not necessary to wear special clothing for this exercise. *Dao-In* is not a social activity. Just wear ordinary, loose clothing. Natural fibers are better because they allow each cell and each pore of your skin to breathe. Synthetic fabrics will cause your energy to rush to the area that is not covered, usually your head. Many people, especially men, dress in formal suits for work. Their bodies have no contact with fresh air, and the places where they work do not have much fresh, clean air either, but the head is still exposed and open to the air. This makes the head congested and nervous and can cause headaches.

This is an interesting phenomenon which is helpful to know about. For example, if you seal off most of the body, leaving only one part exposed, the energy will rush to that part.

I suggest you dress as casually and relaxed as possible when you do *Dao-In*, and in your daily life as well. In ancient times, people dressed in a relaxed way, and natural materials were used. Synthetic fibers only put more stress on the body's natural functions.

The body relies not only on breathing through the nostrils, but on the energy exchange from one's living and working environment. This is important knowledge for energy conductance. *Dao-In*, like other integral physical arts, extends to your daily life. You need to live and work in a beneficial way. I hope that your knowledge of the effects of different energies will serve your life better.

Here are some additional suggestions and guidelines for your practice.

1. If you practice *Dao-In* seriously, you need to prepare yourself in three ways before beginning to exercise.

A. Do not do it when you are under time pressure. If you try to hurry, you will stress your nervous system, and the exercise will not be beneficial.

B. Be physically clean internally. You need to go to the toilet so there is no pressure on your bladder or rectum.

C. Let go of any disturbing thoughts so that you can practice with a pure, child-like mind. Just enjoy doing it and think of nothing else.

2. In doing any of these movements, consider your personal characteristics and fitness. If the movements are inappropriate for your body type, build or physical strength, the result could be the opposite of what you wish. Energy conducting is not army training. It serves you best when you do it according to your own self-knowledge, understanding, and external conditions, such as the type of work you do, the climate you live in, your physique and your stamina.

3. The last movement of #7, the Immortal Lifts the Mountain, strengthens your body connection through the neck. It especially needs to be done with caution against neck injury.

4. If you have a hard time getting up in the morning and being active, do the Concluding Section first, then do the Main Section, then do the Preliminary Section, which is optional.

5. If you have high blood pressure, avoid any movement which concerns energy rising to the head. That includes movements which involve touching or turning the head or upper body.

6. Even people whose blood pressure is normal should not overdo movements connected with the head. If any movements cause dizziness or a feeling that your head is heavier than other parts of your body, change or stop the frequency and amount of your practice.

7. Some movements are connected with developing the middle part of the body. Do not overdo them unless you do not care if, after many years of practice, you become shaped like an olive or an American football. Moving energy to that part of the body will create that type of shape, whether through exercise or overeating.

8. Although all the movements can help build your strength, do not do them during a period when you are sexually very active. I suggest that you rarify your physical pleasure if you are doing *Dao-In*. Otherwise there will be no benefit. In fact, it can be damaging if you do some of the more strenuous movements.

9. These movements can adjust different tendencies toward imbalance. Young people, or other people who have lots of illusions, can correct their habit of fantasizing by doing any kind of physical arts, such as fencing or oriental martial arts.

10. The purpose of this set of *Dao-In* movements is to refine your sexual energy into *chi*. *Chi* is an energy that is between physical strength and spiritual energy. If you do *Dao-In* correctly and properly, you may obtain health and longevity. The examples of the ancient ones' longevity is proof of that. But *Dao-In* is still not the practice which develops your spiritual sensitivity to know the future or things which are happening many miles away. Those who pursue spiritual immortality and spiritual potency need to do other practices, meditation in particular, as well as *Dao-In*. Physical longevity, spiritual powers and immortality are side

effects of being and living with the Integral Way and of practicing the ancient arts of mental, physical and spiritual self-development.

11. For those who wish to achieve proficiency in martial arts, the Preliminary Section can build a good foundation or serve as an auxiliary practice to your martial arts movement for physical strength.

12. *Dao-In* is not designed to build muscles or physical strength. After practicing *Dao-In* for a period of years, your energy will be too refined for rough, physical, or strenuous work. If heavy or strenuous physical work is your profession, and you cannot change it, you may practice *Dao-In* to help your body, but the effect will be on a level other than the physical level. In order to build muscle, gymnastic work-outs and other types of sports are more suitable than *Dao-In*.

13. In the Preliminary Section, some movements are connected with the middle part of the body. If you can do them, be cautious and gentle to avoid damaging the spine. They are supposed to help the spine to some extent, but it depends on how you manage it. These movements were adopted from the *Dao-In* of Pong Tzu who, legend says, lived for 800 years. There are many different movements adopted from different highly achieved masters. However, only you know your personal physical condition. Observe it carefully and do only what you can enjoy.

14. In the Main Section, you can sit on a mat or a chair but not on a sofa or anything that supports your back, unless it is necessary. The spine should be relaxed. It can be slightly curved like a released bow with both ends naturally tipped forward a little, but do not allow it to be like a pulled bow or an "S." That will cause damage. If your spine already has some trouble like

that, try to straighten it as required in *Dao-In* or any good sitting posture.

The reason spiritual evolution occurred internally in humans is that the internal organs communicate through the spinal cord to the head, which receives energy from the sky. Then the sky energy moves downward to the whole body.

15. *Dao-In* should be done in total relaxation. It is best done in the early morning when your stomach is empty. The purpose is to invigorate your energy. If your stomach has anything in it, the effect will be different.

16. It is preferable to do *Dao-In* during the morning, because from midnight to noon is the cycle of the rising sun. Sundown is usually not the best choice, but for modern life, you should do it before the early evening. If you do *Dao-In* too late, your internal energy will be surfing, and it will be hard for you to relax at night in preparation for sleep.

17. If you like physical activity such as sports and games, it is important to protect your muscles, tendons, bones and joints. I do not mean damage from an improper way of moving or an external situation. You need to protect yourself from wind, water and cold, especially during cold and damp seasons. Otherwise, worse trouble can happen to your arms and legs or other parts of the body. Take care of any kind of spasm, pain or numbness before it develops further. Even if you practice Integral Physical Arts such as *t'ai chi* or *Dao-In*, this physical protection cannot be neglected.

18. Unless a specific problem needs to be addressed by repeating a single movement for several days or months, the whole *Dao-In* set needs to be practiced in order to develop yourself in a balanced way. It is not beneficial to do only one movement or posture.

Important Guidance for Practicing Dao-In 29

You need to exercise the whole body. If you do one thing repeatedly, it becomes mechanical and does not help your spiritual development or balanced physical development. So do not overdo any of the movements, but seek your own balanced development by doing all of them or a group of them.

The movements I give in this book are fundamental. They are essential for most people in general daily life. There are deeper levels to the art of *Dao-In* which require specific devotion.

19. Be careful. Some *Dao-In* postures require more training of certain muscles. Moving into a posture too suddenly may cause trouble or pain. To avoid this, build up your practice very gradually. If you are not doing this under the guidance of an instructor, you have to be self-responsible and make good choices by expanding your knowledge.

Chapter 5

Dao-In:
The Integral Way
of Conducting Energy in the Body

PRELIMINARY SECTION - PART I

#1 The Immortal Awakening from Napping

Beginning Posture: Lie on back with legs straight, feet apart. Arms are straight and rest naturally alongside the body, palms up (Figure 1).

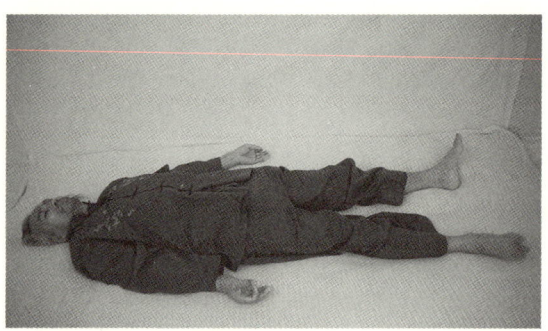

(Figure 1)

1. Bring feet together.

2. Inhaling, slowly raise head and shoulders until the shoulder blades clear the floor. At the same time, bring the palms alongside the body to touch the outside of the thigh.

3. Bring the chin down toward the chest and gaze at toes (Figure 2). This will connect the body's energy in a circle from head to toe.

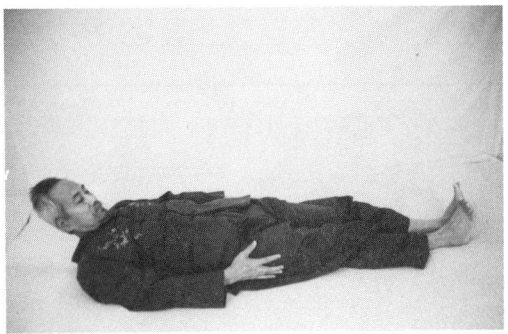

(Figure 2)

4. Exhaling, reverse the movement to return to the beginning posture.

5. Repeat steps 1 - 4 for a total of three times.

Note: This exercise may be done as a single movement 12 to 36 times as a special practice.
● Follow the principle of "movement within stillness" and do this exercise in a very quiet, relaxed manner.
● Avoid sitting up too high. This could cause the abdominal muscle to overdevelop.
● Breathe deeply into the lower abdomen.

#2 <u>**Immortal Straightening the Leg**</u>

Beginning Posture: Lie on back with legs straight. Feet are apart and arms are straight and rest naturally alongside the body, palms up (same as Figure 1).

1. Inhaling, bend left knee, folding the left leg up to the chest.

2. Clasp bent leg with hands; fingers are interlaced. Body should be relaxed with head on floor (Figure 3).

32 Attune Your Body with Dao-In

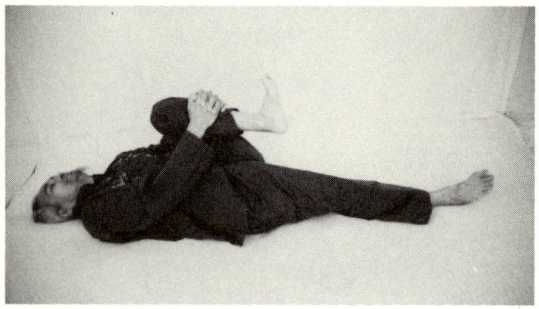

(Figure 3)

3. Exhaling, circle foot at ankle 5 times clockwise and 5 times counter-clockwise.

4. Inhaling, straighten the knee so the leg is straight up, perpendicular to the floor.

5. Exhaling, gently and slowly lower the straight leg to the floor and return to the beginning posture.

Instructions for Opposite Side

6. Inhaling, bend right knee, folding the right leg up to the chest.

7. Clasp bent leg with hands; fingers are interlaced. Body should be relaxed with head on floor.

8. Exhaling, circle foot at ankle 5 times clockwise and 5 times counter-clockwise.

9. Inhaling, straighten the knee so the leg is straight up, perpendicular to the floor.

10. Exhaling, gently and slowly lower the straight leg to the floor and return to beginning posture.

Note: This movement may be done once or repeated 3 times.

#3 Immortal Imitating Butterfly Opening Its Wings

Beginning Posture: Lie on back (Figure 1)

1. Inhaling, bend left knee, folding the left leg up to the chest.

2. Exhaling, clasp bent leg with hands; fingers are interlaced. Body should be relaxed with head on floor (Figure 3).

3. Inhaling, gently and slowly raise the head to the left knee (Figure 4).

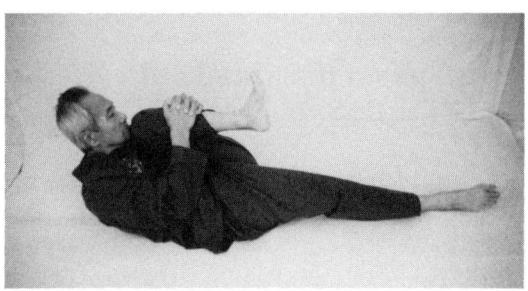

(Figure 4)

4. Exhaling, slowly lower the head. Left leg remains in bent position, clasped by hands.

5. Repeat steps 3 and 4 for a total of 3 times.

6. Inhaling, straighten the knee so the leg is straight up, perpendicular to the floor.

7. Exhaling, slowly lower the straight leg to the floor and return to the beginning posture.

Instructions for Opposite Side

8. Inhaling, bend right knee, folding the right leg up to the chest.

9. Exhaling, clasp bent leg with hands; fingers are interlaced. Head should be on the floor.

10. Inhaling, gently raise the head to the right knee.

11. Exhaling, slowly lower the head. Right leg remains in bent position, clasped by hands.

12. Repeat steps 10 and 11 for a total of 3 times.

13. Inhaling, straighten the knee so the leg is straight up, perpendicular to the floor.

14. Exhaling, slowly lower the straight leg to the floor and return to the beginning posture.

Further instruction

15. Inhaling, bend both knees folding both legs up toward chest.

16. Exhaling, clasp bent legs with hands; fingers are interlaced. Body should be relaxed with head on floor.

17. Inhaling, gently and slowly raise head to knees. (Figure 5).

(Figure 5)

18. Exhaling, slowly lower the head. Legs remain clasped by hands.

19. Repeat Steps 17 and 18 for a total of 3 times.

20. Inhaling, place hands on knees and straighten knees; legs are straight up, perpendicular to the floor (Figure 6).

(Figure 6)

21. Exhaling, bend knees; hands remain on knees.

22. Inhaling, straighten legs.

23. Exhaling, gently lower the legs.

24. Return to beginning posture.

#4 **Immortal Tightening the Body Like a Bow**

Beginning Posture: Lie on back with legs straight (Figure 1).

1. Bring hands to chest.

2. Inhaling, slowly raise the straight legs and the torso so the body forms a "V", at the same time moving the hands to touch the toes. The tailbone is the only part touching the floor (Figure 7).

(Figure 7)

3. Exhaling, slowly return to beginning posture.

4. Repeat steps 1 - 3 for a total of 3 times.

Note: Gradually work toward being able to hold yourself in the raised position for one minute.

#5 Immortal Imitating Grazing Horse Raising Its Head

Beginning Posture: Lie on back (Figure 1)

1. Gently raise and lower left knee.

2. Gently raise and lower right knee.

3. Inhaling, raise the torso (as in a sit-up) moving the hands (arms are straight) down to the ankles.

4. Rock forward and back from the hips. The palms move from ankle to toes and back, massaging feet. Breathe naturally.

5. Repeat step 4 for a total of 9 times.

6. Return to beginning posture and relax.

Note: Breathe deeply and slowly.

#6 Immortal Embracing the Universe

Beginning Posture: Lie on back (Figure 1)

1. Bring both arms across the chest. Hands hold the opposite upper arm, as if embracing oneself, giving the back and shoulders a good stretch.

2. Inhaling, raise torso so the shoulder blades and head are not touching the ground.

3. Remaining in the raised position, bring the chin to the chest, then turn the head to the left and circle the head back. Then reverse the path to return the head to the front. Circle the head to the right in the same manner. Then turn the head in all directions (Figure 8).

38 Attune Your Body with Dao-In

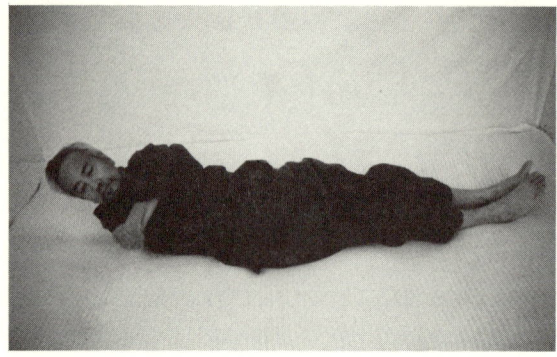

(Figure 8)

4.   Exhaling, return to beginning posture.

#7 **Immortal Lifting the Mountain**

Beginning Posture: Lie on back (Figure 1).

1.   Bring the feet back, close to the buttocks.

2.   Inhaling, slowly raise the hips, keeping the feet, head, neck and shoulders on the floor. Hands should be on the floor, parallel to the body (Figure 9).

(Figure 9)

3. Exhaling, gently lower the body.

4. Repeat steps 2 and 3 for a total of 3 times.

5. Place hands on lower abdomen, slightly above groin (Figure 10).

(Figure 10)

6. Inhaling, raise entire body so it is supported only by the top of the head and the feet (Figure 11).

(Figure 11)

7. Exhaling, gently lower the body.

8. Repeat steps 6 and 7 for a total of 3 times.

40 Attune Your Body with Dao-In

9. Return to beginning posture.

10. Pull the feet slightly in toward the body (4-5" only).

11. Inhaling, gently raise the body so it is supported only by the heels, head, elbows and forearms. Palms should be down (Figure 12).

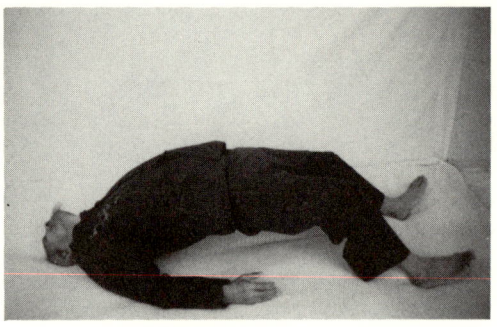

(Figure 12)

12. Exhaling, gently lower the body, allowing the palms to turn upward.

13. Repeat steps 11 and 12 for a total of 3 times.

14. Return to beginning posture and relax.

Note: Steps 6 and 7, 11 and 12, which strengthen your body connection through the neck, need to be done with special caution against neck injury.

PRELIMINARY SECTION - PART II

#8 The Immortal Imitating the Owl Turning Its Head

Beginning Posture: Sit with both legs straight in front.

1. Bend left leg, place sole of foot on the inside of right thigh, near the groin.

2. Place palms of both hands on the outside of right knee, several inches apart, with left hand nearest the right foot.

3. Inhaling, turn the head and torso to the right and look up. Bend forward.

4. Exhaling, turn back to face front and relax. Keep hands on leg.

5. Move the left or both hands down to outside of the calf.

6. Repeat steps 3 and 4.

7. Move the left or both palms to the outside of the ankle (Figure 13).

(Figure 13)

8. Repeat steps 3 and 4.

9. Return to beginning posture and relax.

<u>*Instructions for Opposite Side*</u>

10. Bend right leg, place sole of foot on the inside of the left thigh, near the groin.

11. Place palms of both hands on outside of left knee, several inches apart, with right hand nearest left foot.

12. Inhaling, turn head and torso left and look up.

13. Exhaling, turn back to front and relax. Keep hands on leg.

14. Move the right or both hands down to outside of the calf.

15. Repeat steps 12 and 13.

16. Move the right or both palms to outside of ankle.

17. Repeat steps 12 and 13.

18. Return to beginning posture and relax.

#9 **Immortal Imitating Bamboo Bending in the Wind**

Beginning Posture: Sit with both legs straight in front.

1. Inhaling, bend left leg, place sole of foot on inside of right thigh, near the groin.

2. Exhaling, bend forward placing hands on toes, allowing head to touch right knee.

3. Inhaling, raise the chin up, still grasping the top of the foot.

4. Repeat Steps 2 and 3 for a total of 3 times.

5. Return to beginning posture.

Instructions for Opposite Side

6. Inhaling, bend right leg, place sole of foot on inside of right thigh, near the groin.

7. Exhaling, bend forward placing hands on toes, allowing head to touch left knee.

8. Inhaling, raise the chin up, still grasping top of foot (Figure 14).

(Figure 14)

9. Repeat steps 7 and 8 for a total of 3 times.

10. Return to beginning posture.

Note: Keep movements steady and even.

#10 Immortal Imitating a Sea Lion Raising Its Head

Beginning Posture: Sit with both legs straight in front.

1. Inhaling, bend left leg, place sole of foot on inside of right thigh, near the groin.

2. Grasp middle of the sole of the right foot with right hand; grasp toes of right foot with left hand.

3. Exhaling, gently pull head to right knee turning the head so the right ear is over the knee. Twist body left.

4. Without letting go of the foot, rock up and down 3 times.

5. Inhaling, return to beginning posture.

Instructions for Opposite Side

6. Inhaling, bend right leg, place sole of foot on inside of right thigh, near the groin.

7. Grasp middle of the sole of the left foot with the left hand; grasp the toes of left foot with right hand.

8. Exhaling, gently pull head to left knee, turning the head so the left ear is over the knee. Twist body right (Figure 15).

9. Without letting go of the foot, rock up and down 3 times.

10. Return to beginning posture.

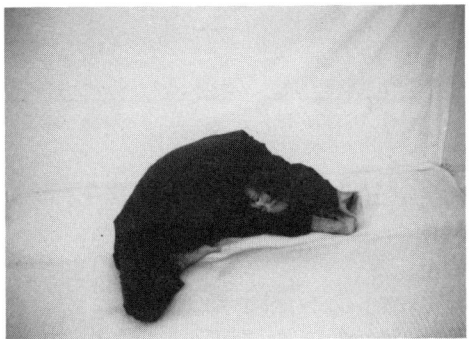

(Figure 15)

#11 Immortal Imitating a Blue Jay Looking Behind Him

Beginning Posture: Sit with both legs straight in front.

1. Inhaling, bend left leg, place sole of foot on the inside of the right thigh near the groin.

2. Place the left hand on the left knee and grasp the top of the right foot with the right hand.

3. Exhaling, lower the body and place the right ear on the right knee.

4. Inhaling, without changing the position of the hands, raise up.

5. Exhaling, lower the body and touch the left knee with the nose.

6. Inhaling, without changing the position of the hands, raise up.

7. Repeat steps 3 - 5 for a total of 3 times.

46 *Attune Your Body with Dao-In*

8. Return to beginning posture.

Instructions for Opposite Side

9. Inhaling, bend right leg, place sole of foot on inside of right thigh, near groin.

10. Place right hand on right knee and grasp the top of left foot with left hand.

11. Exhaling, lower the body and place left ear on left knee.

12. Inhaling, without changing position of the hands, raise up.

13. Exhaling, lower the body and touch the left knee with the nose.

14. Inhaling, without changing hand positions, raise up.

15. Repeat steps 10 - 13 for a total of 3 times.

16. Return to beginning posture.

PRELIMINARY SECTION - PART III

#12 Immortal Imitating the Lazy Tiger Stretching

Beginning Posture: Lie on stomach in a push-up position, arms bent, hands under the shoulders, chin tilted up.

1. Inhaling, straighten both arms, raising the torso and lifting the chin up. Legs rest on the floor (Figure 16).

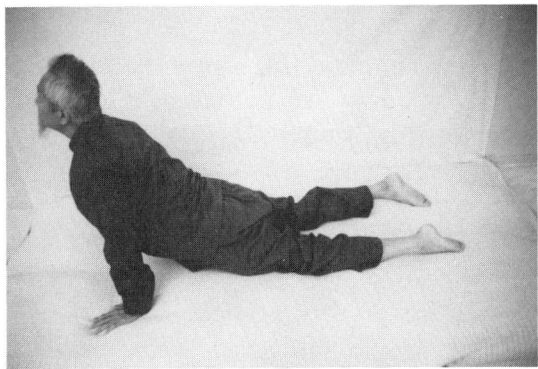

(Figure 16)

2. Exhaling, with arms straight, move the body back, bending the knees until the buttocks are over the feet (Figure 17).

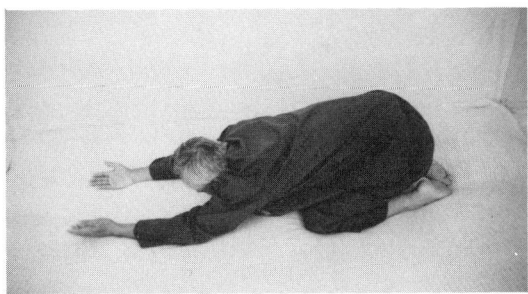

(Figure 17)

48 Attune Your Body with Dao-In

3. Inhaling, move forward with arms straight into position as in Step 1 (Figure 16).

4. Repeat steps 2 and 3 for a total of 3 times.

5. Exhaling, move body half-way back and place forearms on floor. You are now resting on knees and forearms as if crawling.

6. Move off the knees and onto balls of feet.

7. Inhaling, with legs straight, raise buttocks up, bending the body to form an inverted "V". Head should be between elbows (Figure 18).

(Figure 18)

8. Exhaling, lower the body, legs straight, allowing the head to move forward until the body is parallel to the floor. Lift chin up. Do not touch floor with legs.

9. Repeat steps 7 and 8 for a total of 3 times.

10. Inhaling, with legs straight, raise buttocks up, bending the body to form an inverted "V" (Figure 18).

11. Place the head on the floor between the elbows. Slowly shift the weight onto the head.

12. Place hands over tailbone. Clasp hands with palms up. Remain in position approximately 10 seconds and breathe naturally (Figure 19).

(Figure 19)

13. Move hands down by shoulders, palms down on the floor.

14. Inhaling, straighten arms to raise body, legs straight (Figure 20).

(Figure 20)

50 Attune Your Body with Dao-In

15. Bending the knees, lower body onto knees in a crawling position. Hands and feet remain in prior position.

16. Exhaling, with arms straight move body back, bending knees until buttocks are over the feet. (Figure 17).

17. Move the hands forward slightly.

18. Inhaling, shift onto balls of feet, and straightening the arms and legs, raise body to form inverted "V" (Figure 21).

(Figure 21)

19. Exhaling, keeping the legs straight, bend the elbows to lower body to be parallel with the floor as in a low push-up. Then straighten the elbows, arch the back and raise the upper body. Lift chin and look up (Figure 22).

(Figure 22)

20. Inhaling, bend elbows, lower head and upper body to return to low push-up position. Then straightening the arms, raise buttocks up to form an inverted "V". Raise up as high as you can (Figure 21).

21. Repeat steps 18 and 19 for a total of 3 times.

Note: If this movement strains the breath, stop and rest.

#13 Immortal Imitating Peacock Turning and Looking at Tail Feathers

Beginning Posture: Right leg straight behind in line with center of body. Left leg bent up under abdomen; right foot under right buttock. Legs form a straight line down center of body. Arms straight and slightly wider than the shoulders. Upper body raised, look up.

1. Exhaling, bend both elbows, lowering torso straight down to touch right thigh. Then twist to right, placing right ear over the left hand (Figure 23).

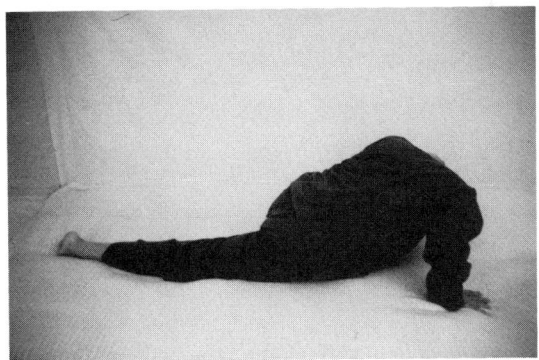

(Figure 23)

2.   Inhaling, return to beginning posture.

52 Attune Your Body with Dao-In

3. Exhaling, bend both elbows, lowering torso straight down. Then twist to the right, placing left ear over right hand and looking back at right foot (Figure 24).

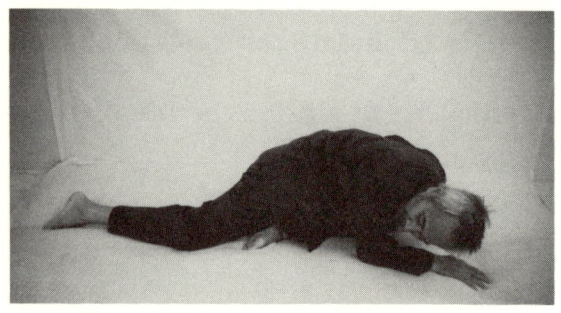

(Figure 24)

4. Inhaling, return to beginning posture.

5. Repeat steps 1 - 4 for a total of 3 times.

<u>*Instructions for Opposite Side*</u>

Beginning Posture: Left leg straight behind in line with center of body. Right leg bent up under abdomen; right foot under right buttock. Legs form straight line. Arms straight and slightly wider than shoulders. Upper body raised, look up.

6. Exhaling, bend both elbows, lowering torso straight down to touch right thigh. Then twist to right, placing left ear over right hand.

7. Inhaling, return to beginning posture.

8. Exhaling, bend both elbows, lowering torso straight down. Then twist to left, placing right ear over left hand and look back at left foot.

Dao-In 53

9. Inhaling, return to beginning posture.

10. Repeat steps 6 - 9 for a total of 3 times.

Note: Move slowly, gently, and gracefully with control.

#14 **The Immortal Stretching Well**

Beginning Posture: Sit with right leg as when crosslegged and left leg turned out to left so that left heel is touching left buttock. Left hand is holding left ankle, right hand is holding right heel.

1. Inhaling, turn head right, twist torso right and lean to right still holding the heel (Figure 25).

(Figure 25)

2. Exhaling, twist head and upper body to the left (Figure 26), and lower the body, bringing the right shoulder to the right knee, still holding ankle (Figure 27).

3. Inhaling, return to beginning posture.

4. Repeat steps 4 - 6 for a total of 3 times.

54 Attune Your Body with Dao-In

(Figure 26)

(Figure 27)

Instructions for Opposite Side

Beginning Posture: Sit with left leg as when crosslegged and right leg turned out to right so that right heel is touching right buttock. Right hand is holding right ankle. Left hand is holding left heel.

5. Exhaling, turn head left, twist torso left and lean to left, still holding the heel.

6. Inhaling, twist head and upper body to right, then exhaling, lower the body bringing the left shoulder to left knee.

7. Inhaling, return to beginning posture.

#15 Immortal Pulling Bow String

Beginning Posture: Lie face down, chin up and head off floor.

1. Place hands behind back over kidneys. Slowly rub spine from kidneys to tailbone and back. Raise chest

slightly as hands move over tailbone; lower when the hands move over kidneys (Figure 28).

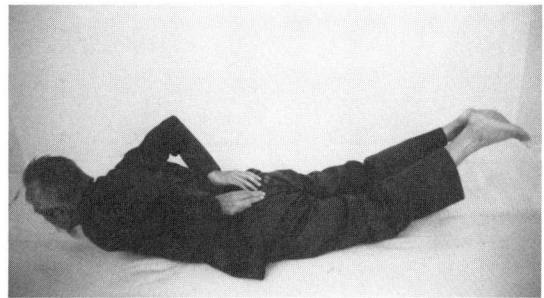

(Figure 28)

2. Repeat step 1 for a total of 3 times.

3. Arch the back, raising the chest and legs off the ground, body resting on lower abdomen and groin.

4. Slowly rub either side of spine with palms, from kidneys over the buttocks and back to the kidneys.

5. Repeat step 4 for a total of 3 times.

6. Straighten both arms and circle out to side and around extended in front of body (Figure 29).

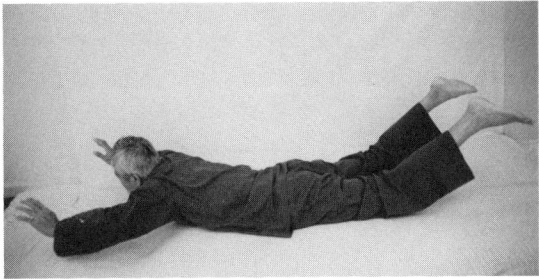

(Figure 29)

7. Hold this position for approximately 10 seconds.

Note: Breathe slowly and naturally.

MAIN SECTION - PART I

This section and the rest of the exercises, taken from different records and ancient books, were most favored by ancient people who live to be over 160 years old.

#16 Immortal Imitating a Tall Pine Standing Firmly in the Wind

Beginning Posture: Sit crosslegged with hands clasped behind head at base of skull. Elbows out to side (Figure 30). (This exercise can also be done sitting with legs out in front.)

(Figure 30)

1. Inhaling, push back with head and forward with arms while bringing elbow around in front of head. This creates polarity pressure.

2. Exhaling, relax and return to beginning posture.

3. Still clasped, move hands midway up the back of the head.

4. Repeat steps 1 and 2.

5. Still clasped, move hands up to the top portion of the back of the head.

6. Repeat Steps 1 and 2.

Note: This movement may be repeated 1, 3, or 5 times in each hand position.
● Stop and rest if you get out of breath.
● It is not suitable to do this exercise at night.
● It is preferable to do it in the early morning when you awaken.

#17 Immortal Imitating a Lizard Turning to Watch a Dragonfly

Beginning Posture: Sit crosslegged with hands clasped behind head. Elbows out to side. (Figure 30)

1. Exhaling, bend forward at the waist and twist the body to the left, bringing the right elbow in line with the center line of the body, slightly lower than the knees.

2. Inhaling, return to the beginning posture.

3. Exhaling, bend forward at the waist twisting the body to the right, bringing the left elbow in line with the center line of the body and slightly lower than knees (Figure 31).

4. Inhaling, return to beginning posture.

5. Exhaling, bend forward at the waist (slightly lower than before) twisting the body to the left, bringing the right elbow in line with the center line of the body and 3 - 5 inches from the floor.

6. Inhaling, return to beginning posture.

(Figure 31)

7. Exhaling, bend forward at the waist, twisting the body to the right, bringing the left elbow in line with the center line of the body 3 - 5 inches from the floor.

8. Inhaling, return to beginning posture.

9. Exhaling, bend forward at the waist, twisting the body left, bringing the right elbow in line with the center line of the body and to the floor.

10. Inhaling, return to beginning posture.

11. Exhaling, bend forward at the waist, twisting body to the right, bringing the left elbow in line with the center line of the body and to the floor.

12. Inhaling, return to beginning posture.

Note: This movement should only be done in the daytime on an empty stomach.

60 Attune Your Body with Dao-In

#18 **Immortal Massaging the Wind Pond Point**

Beginning Posture: Sit crosslegged.

1. Inhaling, massage the depression behind the ears and at the base of the skull with the fingers. Tilt head up slightly (Figure 32).

(Figure 32)

2. Exhaling, continue massaging the point while bending forward at the waist. Tilt head down.

3. Repeat steps 1 and 2 for 30 - 60 seconds.

4. Return to beginning posture.

Note: This point on the head is called "Wind Pond" in Traditional Chinese Medicine.
● Do not do this at night. It may be done in the daytime whenever you feel tired.

#19 **Immortal Beating the Heavenly Drum**

Beginning Posture: Sit crosslegged.

1. Cover both ears with palms, fingers of each hand pointing toward each other at back of head.

2. Inhaling, place index finger on top of middle finger, then snap it off, striking the back of the head on the depression located behind the ears at the base of the skull (Wind Pond point) - (Figure 33). Repeat continuously, approximately one strike per second.

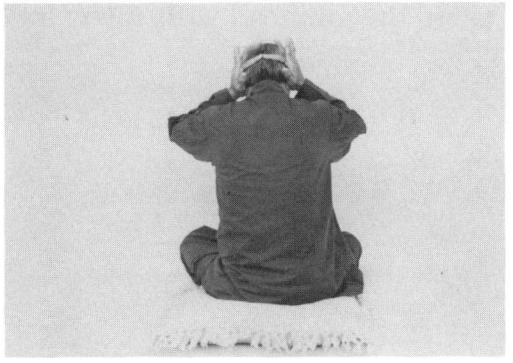

(Figure 33)

3. Exhaling, continue striking with index fingers while bending forward at the waist. Tilt head down.

4. Repeat steps 2 and 3 for 20 - 30 seconds until 36 strikes have been made.

Note: It is best to do this in the morning or daytime, whenever you feel tight in the head. This movement increases cerebral circulation.

#20 **Immortal Sounding the Heavenly Bell**

Beginning Posture: Sit crosslegged.

1. While holding the palms over both ears, create a tight seal and bite the teeth firmly: 9 times in front, on both sides and in back. (total of 36 times)

62 Attune Your Body with Dao-In

Note: This greatly helps maintain the health of the mouth and teeth.

#21 **Immortal Pressing the Sun and Moon Corners**

Beginning Posture: Sit crosslegged.

1. Inhaling, press the forehead with the palms just inside the temples (Figure 34).

(Figure 34)

2. Exhaling, release.

3. Repeat steps 1 and 2 for a total of 3 times.

Note: This movement should be done in the morning or during the day when you head feels stressed by too much thinking.

#22 **Immortal Turning to Look Back**

Beginning Posture: Sit crosslegged.

1. Exhaling, place both hands on right knee, bending forward at the waist. Turn the head to the right and twist

upper body to the right. Press down with hands and push up with knee.

2. Inhaling, return to beginning posture.

3. Exhaling, place both hands on left knee, bending forward at the waist. Turn head to the left and twist upper body to the left. Press down with hands and push up with knee (Figure 35).

(Figure 35)

4. Inhaling, return to beginning posture.

5. Repeat steps 1 - 4 for a total of 3 times.

Note: This movement can be done when you sit too long in meditation, at desk work or on some other similar occasion.

#23 Immortal Imitating a Bird Turning Its Head

Beginning Posture: Sit crosslegged. Make fists and place the knuckles on floor in front of body, elbows bent and body bending at waist to bring head near floor.

64 Attune Your Body with Dao-In

1.   Inhaling, straighten left arm, turn head left to look up, and twist body left.

2.   Exhaling, return to beginning posture.

3.   Inhaling, straighten right arm, turn head right to look up and twist body right. (Figure 36).

(Figure 36)

4.   Repeat steps 1 - 3 for a total of 3 times.

Note: This should only be done as part of the whole *Dao-In* series.

#24 Immortal Shaking the Immortal Peach Tree

Beginning Posture: Right leg bent, with right foot under buttock; left leg bent with left foot in front of right foot. Grasp right thumb with left hand, then cover left fist with right hand and place just below navel (Figure 37).

1.   Move clasped hands up to solar plexus and down again very vigorously 36 times, causing the whole body to shake up and down.

(Figure 37)

Note: Do this only in the morning before eating or drinking as part of the whole *Dao-In* series.

MAIN SECTION - PART II

#25 Immortal Imitating a Bird Washing Its Wings

Beginning Posture: Sit crosslegged. Right arm straight, with right palm on floor next to right hip. Left hand holds right arm, just above elbow (Figure 38).

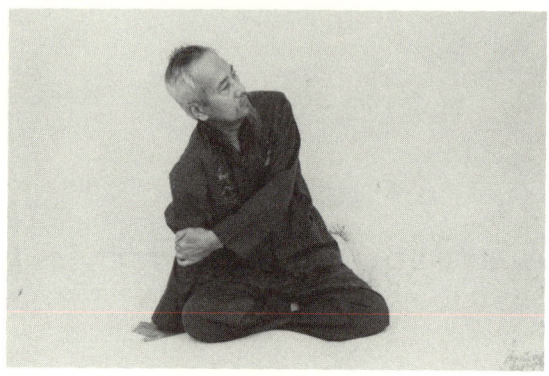

(Figure 38)

1. Inhaling, pull against right arm with left arm. Pull vigorously twisting the body left while resisting the leftward pull with the right side. Pull 5 times. This is a polarity movement.

2. Exhaling, relax.

<u>Instructions for Opposite Side</u>

Beginning Posture: Sit crosslegged, left palm on floor alongside left hip. Right hand holding left arm, just above elbow.

3. Inhaling, pull against left arm with right arm. Pull vigorously, twisting the body right while resisting the rightward pull with the left side. Pull 5 times.

4. Exhaling, relax and return to beginning posture.

Note: This movement should be done along with the whole set only. It is suitable to practice either day or night.

#26 **Dragon Stretching Its Paws**

Beginning Posture: Sit crosslegged.

1. Inhaling, turn head left and stretch both arms out to the right at shoulder height. Push out 3 times from the outstretched position, attaining a good stretch (Figure 39).

(Figure 39)

2. Exhaling, return to beginning posture.

3. Inhaling, turn head right and stretch both arms out to the left at shoulder height. Push out left 3 times from outstretched position, attaining a good stretch.

4. Exhaling, return to beginning posture.

5. Repeat steps 1 - 4 for a total of 3 times.

68 Attune Your Body with Dao-In

Note: This movement should be done along with the whole set only. It is suitable for day or night practice.

#27 **Immortal Stretching the Bow**

Beginning Posture: Sit crosslegged.

1. Inhaling, bring both hands to center chest, elbows out to the sides. Left palm facing away from body and fingers fully bent at the second knuckle. Right thumb and forefinger straight up and other fingers bent at the second knuckle.

2. Twist body to right and down, extending right arm straight up over and behind body. At the same time, the left arm remains bent at the elbow pulling in opposition to the right hand, as if drawing a bow.

3. From the outstretched position, push with the right and pull with the left 3 times, attaining a good stretch (Figure 40). Look at right hand.

(Figure 40)

4. Exhaling, return to beginning posture.

Instructions for Opposite Side:

Beginning Posture: Sit crosslegged.

5. Inhaling, bring both hands to center of chest, elbows out to the sides. Right palm is facing away from body and fingers fully bent at the second knuckle. Left thumb and forefinger straight up and other fingers bent at second knuckle.

6. Twist body to left and down, extending left arm straight up, over and behind body. At the same time, the right arm remains bent at the elbow, pulling in opposition to the left hand as in drawing a bow.

7. From an outstretched position, push with the left and pull with the right hand 3 times, attaining a good stretch.

8. Exhaling, return to beginning posture.

9. Repeat steps 1 - 8 for a total of 3 times.

Note: This movement should be done along with the whole set only. It is suitable for day or night.

#28 Immortal Holding Up the Sky

Beginning Posture: Sit crosslegged. Right arm straight with right palm on floor next to right hip.

1. Inhaling, raise left hand up over head, turning palm up and fingertips pointing to the right. From the outstretched position, push up with the left and down with the right 3 times attaining a good stretch. Look at left hand (Figure 41).

70 Attune Your Body with Dao-In

(Figure 41)

2. Exhaling, return to beginning posture.

Instructions for Opposite Side

Beginning Posture: Sit crosslegged. Left arm straight with left hand palm down on floor, next to left hip.

3. Inhaling, raise right hand up over head, turning palm up and fingertips pointing to the left. From the outstretched position, push up with the right hand and down with the left 3 times, attaining a good stretch. Look at right hand.

4. Exhaling, return to the beginning posture.

5. Repeat steps 1 - 4 for a total of 3 times.

Note: This movement should not be done at night.

#29: Immortal Fortifying the Great Wall

Beginning Posture: Sit crosslegged.

1. Inhaling, raise right arm and bend 90 degrees at the elbow so that right hand is overhead with lightly-clenched fist, palm up. With the left hand in a lightly-clenched fist, strike the right side of the body, palm facing body. Move in a circle on the right side, in center down to waist, to extreme right side, up under arm and to beginning. Inhale, then hold breath while striking 36 times (Figure 42).

(Figure 42)

2. Exhaling, return to beginning posture.

3. Inhaling, raise left arm bending 90 degrees at the elbow so that the left hand is overhead with lightly-clenched fist, palm up. With the right hand in a lightly clenched fist, strike the left side of the body, palm facing body. Move in a circle on the left side, down to waist, to extreme left side, up under arm and back to beginning. Inhale, then hold breath or breathe naturally while striking 36 times.

4. Exhaling, return to beginning posture.

Note: The striking should be hard but not so it hurts. This movement should be done along with the entire set, during daylight, on an empty stomach.

#30 Immortal Turning to Look at the Moon

Beginning Posture: Sit crosslegged with right hand on outside of left knee and left hand behind the back with the back of the hand over the right kidney (Figure 43).

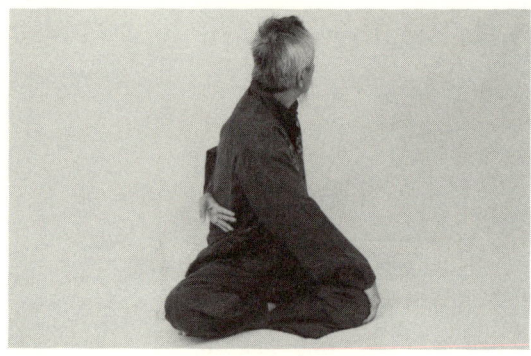

(Figure 43)

1. Inhaling, turn head to the left, pulling torso left with right arm pressure against left knee.

2. Continue inhaling, tilt chin down and then turn head to right, twisting body to the right.

3. Exhaling, return to beginning posture.

4. Repeat steps 1 - 3 for a total of 3 times.

<u>*Instructions for Opposite Side:*</u>

Beginning Posture: Sit crosslegged with left hand on outside of right knee and the right hand behind back with the back of the hand over the left kidney.

5. Inhaling, turn head to the right, pulling torso right with left arm pressure against right knee.

6. Continue inhaling, tilt chin down and then turn head to left, twisting body to the left.

7. Exhaling, return to beginning posture.

8. Repeat steps 1 - 3 for a total of 3 times.

Note: This movement can be done for self-adjustment anytime during the day.

#31 Red Dragon Stirring the Sea

Beginning Posture: Sit crosslegged. Hands, with fingers interlocked, are on back of head.

1. Open mouth wide and stretch the tongue down to try to touch the chin (Figure 44).

(Figure 44)

2. Stretch tongue up to try to touch the nose.

3. Repeat steps 1 and 2 for a total of 3 times.

4. With tongue outside mouth, circle the tongue 3 times in each direction, stretching fully.

74 Attune Your Body with Dao-In

5. Separating accumulated saliva into 3 parts, swallow 3 times deeply into the lower *tan tien* (1-1/2" below the navel.)

Note: This movement should be done in early morning or evening to maintain health of your tongue.

#32 **Slowly Turning the Earth**

Beginning Posture: Sit crosslegged.

1. Place the palms over the kidneys (Figure 45).

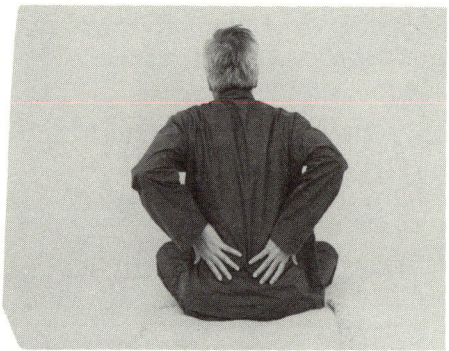

(Figure 45)

2. Massage the area over the kidneys with both palms. Start with the palms on both sides of spine, circle up, then to the outside, circle down, then return to both sides of spine. Repeat 36 times.

Note: This can be done by itself or with the entire set.
● Persons with kidney weakness should increase the number of repetitions.
● It can be done day or night.

MAIN SECTION - PART III

#33 Immortal Turning the Pulley to Raise the Energy

Beginning Posture: Sit crosslegged, arms relaxed, with hands alongside hips.

1. Circle the right shoulder from front to back, 36 times (Figure 46).

(Figure 46)

2. Circle the left shoulder, from front to back, 36 times.

#34 Immortal Imitating a Hummingbird's Flight

Beginning Posture: Sit crosslegged.

1. Place the backs of the hands behind the body on the waist.

2. Circle both shoulders from front to back, 36 times.

3. Circle both shoulders, from back to front, 36 times.

Note: Movements 33 and 34 can be done during the day and are beneficial when the arms and shoulders have

76 Attune Your Body with Dao-In

been overused. They are especially helpful for persons with arthritis or rheumatism and should be done frequently by those affected by these disorders.

#35 **Dragon Dance**

Beginning Posture: Sit crosslegged.

1. Place hands over head, palms together, fingers pointing up. Keep palms together during entire exercise (Figure 47).

(Figure 47)

2. Inhaling, push waist out to the right side while keeping the head and upper torso upright.

3. With right elbow pointing sightly upward, move right elbow fully to the right at shoulder height (Figure 48).

4. Exhaling, push waist out to the left side while keeping the head and upper torso upright.

5. With left elbow pointing slightly upward, move left elbow fully to the left at shoulder height (Figure 49).

(Figure 49)

6. Inhaling, push waist out to right.

7. Follow with right elbow moving right in a position lower than before (Figure 50).

(Figure 50)

78 Attune Your Body with Dao-In

8. Continue this movement from right to left, pushing the waist out, followed by turning from side to side with the elbows. The palms create a swaying movement like a snake or dragon dance, moving gracefully up and down.

Note: Inhale to right, exhale to left.
● This movement helps reduce weight, burning body fat from the waist and stomach.
● This movement should be done during the day on an empty stomach.
● By holding hands below the head, this movement may be done at anytime except just before sleeping.
● Begin slowly and increase speed and vigor, warming up the whole body, but not to the point of perspiration.

#36 <u>**Immortal Imitating the Descending Stars**</u>

Beginning Posture: Sit crosslegged with hands forming fists on the ground alongside hips.

1. Inhaling, straighten the arms, raising the buttocks off the ground (Figure 51).

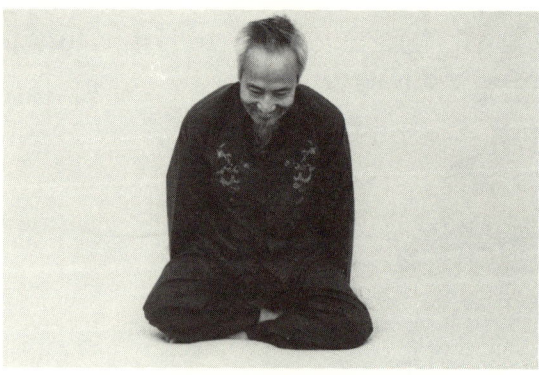

(Figure 51)

2. Exhaling, pull the arms up quickly, dropping the body on the ground abruptly, causing a healthy gentle shock to the body.

3. Repeat 5 times.

Note: This movement is beneficial for those who meditate a lot.
● Do it during the daytime with the whole group of movements.

#37 Immortal Imitating Wind Dispersing the Clouds

Beginning Posture: Sit crosslegged with both arms across the chest so that each hand is on the opposite shoulder.

1. Exhaling, lower chin to chest and bend slightly forward.

2. Inhaling, turn head to the right, circling the head right to tilt back. Straighten the body up (Figure 52).

(Figure 52)

80 Attune Your Body with Dao-In

3. Exhaling, reverse the path to return to front. Lower chin to chest and bend forward.

4. Inhaling, turn head to left, circling the head left to tilt back. Straighten body up.

5. Exhaling, reverse the path to return to front. Lower chin to chest and bend forward.

6. Repeat steps 2 - 5 for a total of 3 times.

Note: This movement should be done during the day.
- Do not do it in evening before sleeping.
- Avoid straining the muscles of the neck.

#38 **Immortal Strengthening the Pillars**

Beginning Posture: Sit with both legs straight in front.

1. Inhaling, place both hands on right knee.

2. Exhaling, press down on knee with hands while resisting the downward pressure by pressing up with right knee. Push down 7 times, once each second (Figure 53).

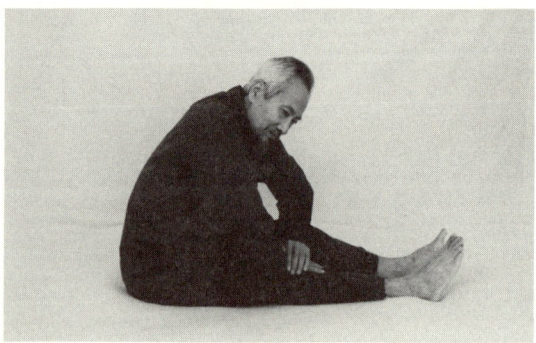

(Figure 53)

3. Inhaling, place both hands on left knee.

4. Exhaling, press down on left knee with hands while resisting the downward pressure by-pressing up with left knee. Push down 7 times, once each second.

5. Inhaling, place left hand on left knee and right hand on right knee.

6. Exhaling, press down on both knees while resisting by pressing up with knees. Push down 7 times, once each second.

7. Rub the knees 36 times with right hand on right knee moving in a counter-clockwise direction and left hand on left knee, moving clockwise.

8. Rub the knees 36 times in opposite directions (right hand moving clockwise; left moving counter clockwise).

Note: This can be done any time.
- It is good when the legs have been overused.

#39 Immortal Watching Twin Flying Horses Scratching Each Other

Beginning Posture: Sit with both legs straight in front. Arms straight and placed behind the body, palms on the floor. Upper body leaning back at a 45 degree angle with arms supporting.

1. With the bottom of the right foot, rub the top of the left foot up and down, from the ankle to the toes, 36 times. (Figure 54).

(Figure 54)

2. With the bottom of the left foot, rub the top of the right foot up and down, from the ankle to the toes, 36 times.

3. With the heel of the right foot, rub the sole of the left foot, from heel to base of toes, 36 times (Figure 55).

(Figure 55)

4. With the heel of the left foot, rub the sole of the right foot, 36 times.

Note: This movement may be done at any time and is especially beneficial to do just before sleeping.

#40 Immortal Beating the Round Drum

Beginning Posture: Sit crosslegged.

1. With both hands in lightly clenched fists, pound the back, striking all parts of the back that can be reached. Hit firmly and evenly, 36 times while breathing deeply (Figure 56).

(Figure 56)

(Figure 57)

2. With the right hand forming a lightly clenched fist, use the palm side of the hand to pound on the front of the body, circling from the left side, then up; down the right side, and then down to the navel and returning to the left. Continue circling, striking 36 times (Figure 57).

3. In the same manner, strike the body 36 times with the left hand circling in the same direction.

Note: Movements 39 and 40 should start by holding the breath.

84 Attune Your Body with Dao-In

- Slowly build up the practice and breathe naturally.
- Do these during the daytime.

#41 Immortal Opening the Heavenly Gate

Beginning Posture: Sit crosslegged.

1. With the hands in lightly clenched fists, pump the arms back, keeping the forearms close to the body. Pump back vigorously in a swinging motion as if striking to the rear with the elbows. Repeat 36 times (Figure 58).

(Figure 58)

Note: This movement should be done with the whole set during the daytime.

- It is most beneficial done vigorously.

MAIN SECTION - PART IV

#42 Immortal Imitating the Wriggle of the Young Dragon

Beginning Posture: Sit with left leg straight in front. Right leg bent at the knee with right foot on floor alongside left knee. Arms straight and placed behind the body, palms on the floor, upper body leaning back at a 45 degree angle with arms supporting (Figure 59).

(Figure 59)

1. Inhaling, lift the body, raising the buttocks as high as possible. Tilt the head back.

2. Exhaling, return to beginning posture.

3. Repeat steps 1 and 2 for a total of 7 times.

<u>Instructions for Opposite Side</u>

Beginning Posture: Sit with right leg straight in front. Left leg bent at the knee with left foot on floor alongside. Arms straight and placed behind body, palms on floor.

86 Attune Your Body with Dao-In

4. Inhaling, lift body, raising buttocks as high as possible. Tilt head back.

5. Exhaling, return to beginning posture.

6. Repeat steps 1 and 2 for a total of 7 times.

7. Still leaning back on arms, place both legs straight in front.

8. Inhaling, lift body, raising buttocks as high as possible. Tilt head back (Figure 60).

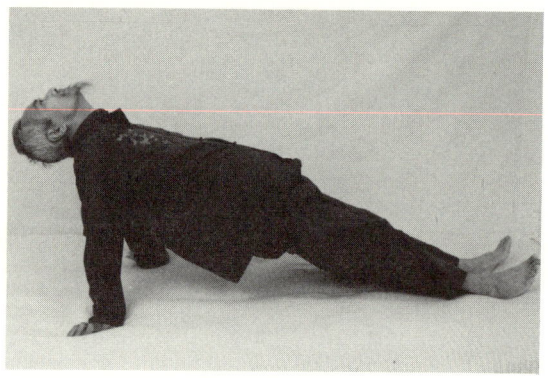

(Figure 60)

9. Exhaling, lower body.

10. Repeat steps 5 and 6 to make a total of 7 times.

Note: This movement should be done with the whole set in the daytime.

#43 The Immortal's Delight

Beginning Posture: Sit with left leg straight in front and right leg bent at the knee with the right foot on the floor along the outside of the left leg.

1. Place both hands on right knee, pulling right leg into body.

2. Inhaling, turn head right and fully twist body right, rubbing the abdomen against the right thigh as you turn (Figure 61).

(Figure 61)

3. Exhaling, turn head left and fully twist body left, rubbing abdomen against the right thigh as you turn.

4. Repeat steps 2 and 3 for a total of 5 times.

Instructions for Opposite Side.

Beginning Posture: sitting with right leg straight in front and left leg bent at the knee with left foot on the floor alongside the outside of the right leg.

5. Place both hands on left knee, pulling left leg into body.

6. Inhaling, turn head left and fully twist body left, rubbing the abdomen against the left thigh as you turn (Figure 62).

88 Attune Your Body with Dao-In

(Figure 62)

7. Exhaling, turn head right and fully twist body right, rubbing abdomen against left thigh as you turn.

Note: This should be done in the morning along with the whole set on an empty stomach.

- It is not suitable for nighttime.
- The movement may be repeated for a total of 36 times.

#44 **Immortal Holding the Foot to Strengthen the Knee**

Beginning Posture: Sit with left leg straight in front and right leg bent at knee, right foot close to right buttock. Hands are under right foot, fingers interlocked.

1. Exhaling, straighten the right leg with hands still clasped under foot (Figure 63).

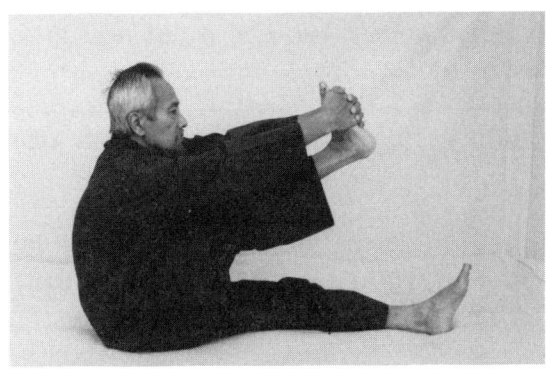

(Figure 63)

2. Inhaling, return to beginning posture.

3. Repeat steps 1 and 2 for a total of 5 times.

Instructions for Opposite Side

Beginning Posture: sitting with right leg straight in front and left leg bent at knee, left foot close to left buttock. Hands are under left foot, fingers interlaced.

4. Exhaling, straighten left leg with hands still clasped under foot.

5. Inhaling, return to beginning posture.

6. Repeat steps 4 and 5 for a total of 5 times.

Note: This may be done with the whole set or by itself.
● Do not do this movement at night.

#45 Immortal Bowing to the Rising Sun

Beginning Posture: sitting with both legs straight in front.

1. Exhaling, bend forward at the waist and grasp the top of both feet with the hands.

2. Inhaling, still holding the feet, raise body up and tilt head up.

3. Exhaling, bend forward and begin making large circles with the feet; right counter-clockwise and left foot clockwise (Figure 64).

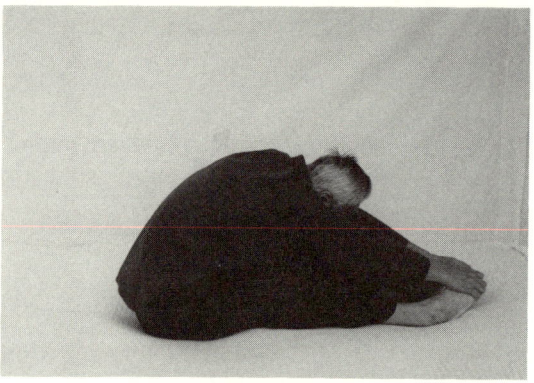

(Figure 64)

4. Inhaling and exhaling naturally, continue circling the feet 21 times. Then reverse the direction of the circles, right clockwise and left counter-clockwise and circle 21 times.

Note: This should be done a part of the whole set and can be done at night.

#46 Immortal Pressing Kun Lun Mountain

Beginning Posture: Sit crosslegged.

1. Interlace fingers of both hands and place the hands behind the head, palms down. Lean forward.

2. Inhaling, with fingers interlaced, push hands straight up overhead, palms up, arms fully extended. Look up at hands.

3. Exhaling, lean forward and lower hands so they are at the back of the neck, palms down.

4. Repeat steps 2 and 3 for a total of 3 times.

5. Place hands, with fingers still interlocked, palm down on top of the head.

6. Inhaling, then holding the breath, press down with the hands and up with the head. Hold ten seconds (Figure 65).

(Figure 65)

7. Exhaling, relax with hands interlocked on top of the head.

8. Repeat steps 6 and 7 for a total of 3 times.

Note: This movement should be done with the whole set in the early morning.
● Do not do it at night because it moves energy upward, causing restless sleep.

- Do not overdo movements connected with the head, especially if you have high blood pressure.

#47 Immortal Stimulating the Scalp

Beginning Posture: Sit crosslegged.

1. Rub the scalp with both hands several times.

2. Place the left hand on back of the head, palm against head.

3. Place right hand on back of head, palm against head. Place left hand on top of head, palm down and rub top of head 36 times in circular motion, counter-clockwise for men and clockwise for women.

Note: Absolutely do not do this exercise in evening or at night.

#48 Immortal Turning the Gristwheel

Beginning Posture: Sit crosslegged.

1. With the left arm behind the back, make small circles with the palm of the right hand over the navel. Circle 36 times clockwise (Figure 66).

2. With the right arm behind the back, make small circles with the palm of the right hand over the navel. Circle 36 times counter-clockwise.

Note: This movement should be done with the whole set.

- It is particularly beneficial before sleep.

(Figure 66)

#49 Immortal in Sitting Meditation

Beginning Posture: Sit crosslegged with back of the hands on thighs, index finger and thumb touching tip to tip and other fingers naturally straight.

After finishing the set of movements of *Dao-In*, there are two ways to practice meditation. They can be done together or separately.

The first is to visualize a fire starting in the perineum and burning upwards inside and outside. You visualize it and feel the warmth *evenly* everywhere in your physical body, internally and externally. This is a traditional practice entitled, "Burning the Body With True Fire." You can use it in your conceptual work of self-forgiveness to let your negative thoughts, bad habits, past mistakes and illnesses be burned away by fire. Use it to burn away your foolishness, stubbornness and prejudice. After that, calm yourself down to a stage of self-forgetting, which means to forget your own existence. Remain in this stage for as long or short a time as you spontaneously wish. Then do some small movements like rubbing your face or rubbing your body to finish the meditation and bring yourself back to daily life.

Instruction for Meditation: Sit on a cushion about 4 inches thick. Your spine should be gently straight. Sit crosslegged with the left leg in front of the folded right leg. The left ankle should be under your right calf and the right ankle behind the left calf to allow both ankle bones some distance. The ankles should not be above one another. The posture is called "Single Folding." The eyelids are gently lowered and the focus is in the direction of the nose with gentle concentration.

A person with an active mind can count the breath. A person who is overly strong physically should only pay attention to and count the exhalations. A weak type of person should only count the inhalations. Advanced practitioners should use only one nostril. During the day, one should use only the left nostril, and at night only use the right nostril.

There are many ways to help you concentrate. Make sure not to let the technique which helps you enter complete concentration, carry you away. The invocations in the *Workbook for Spiritual Development* can be used selectively. You may use just one sentence, half a sentence or a word, repeating them at the beginning of your sitting, before you enter complete concentration. The choice of what is used to center you should be made according to your own spiritual response.

The hand position varies according to age and purpose. Older people who are less active sexually will find it safe to put both hands together, left hand holding the right thumb and the four fingers of the right hand covering the left fist. Gently place the positioned hands in front of the lower *tan tien*, slightly below the navel. For young spiritual people, it is always safe and beneficial to use the position in the middle *tan tien*, a little lower than the front of the spiritual heart center. It is advised to use the hand posture of placing the two thumbprints together and pointing upwards, and the fingers touching, back to back and pointing to the heart center. This is a good hand position for a person with nervous weakness, no matter what their age.

There are three key points of bodily energy on the back of the body and three on the front. On the back, they are on the spine: (1) the point by the kidneys, (2) the point by the spiritual heart and (3) the point at the base of the skull. On the front, they are on the midline: (1) the sexual center in the lower abdomen (2) the spiritual heart and (3) the forehead, which is the spiritual center. Their respective purposes are associated with different spirits.

In this meditation, all six points can be reduced to three centers, and the three centers can be consolidated into one complete focus for a better, gentle concentration. The energy should be transported smoothly anywhere as directed by the mind. The ancient instruction says that the three locations in front and the three locations in the back must finally be gathered as one. If in spiritual self cultivation one can light all of them up, one has found the universal spiritual authority.

Good concentration should last from 3 to 5 minutes. If you have time, you can meditate separately from the exercises. *Dao-In* requires short but complete concentration without forcing oneself. The length of time spent in meditation depends on natural spiritual necessity. Being indulgent in overly long meditation without a positive purpose is not productive. Never do sitting meditation when your mind is too active or disturbed. You can also utilize the meditation instruction in my other books, choosing what you need in order to achieve the different purposes described.

The purpose of the different meditation postures is to assist various energy transformations and spiritual confirmations. The postures can help converge and nurture your spiritual energy. Each individual has the freedom to adjust their personal, physical energy during quiet sitting cultivation.

1. Divine One of Wholeness (Figure 67)

96 Attune Your Body with Dao-In

(Figure 67)

*Remove distraction from the ears and eyes
     to keep your energy full,
     your spirit whole.
Keep the mind from wandering;
     the subtle body is like nature and heaven,
     it receives all and holds nothing.*

2. Divine One of Subtle Integration (Figure 68)

(Figure 68)

*The mind and the heart represent
     the fire energy in our bodies;*

*Only when they are harmonized with the body,
  the water energy,
  can the correct goal
  of fundamental cultivation,
  good health, be achieved.*

3. Divine One of Peaceful-Mindedness (Not pictured) Same as Figure 68 except palms face each other.

   *Flowing smooth and free,
     so should the mind be
     kept clear of sticky impediments,
     keeping the same innocence inside as out.
   This is the way to wholeness.*

4. Divine One of Perfect Harmony (Not pictured) Arms straight in front about shoulder height. Elbows slightly bent, fingers naturally facing forward.

   *The calm power derived from your daily practice
     can transform what seems to be a disaster
     into a blessing.
   Learn this and you will be qualified
     to sit in the seat of the Lotus,
     to look deep within yourself.*

5. Divine One of Equal Mindedness (Figure 69)

(Figure 69)

*To become one with Tao,
   there is one, and only one requirement:
   keep a consistently calm mind.
Keep it peaceful, transparent,
   still as the water of a clear, quiet lake,
   and you will enjoy the subtlety of great bliss.*

6. Divine One of Constant Subtle Virtue (Figure 70)

(Figure 70)

*Stay whole, stay clean, stay firm,
   and in one moment you can experience
   everything of Tao,
   and become an adored child of heaven.*

7. Divine One of Original Simplicity (Not pictured) Arms in front with palms down, elbows slightly bent and hands just below solar plexus.

*Before touching the formed,
   one rests in the unformed.
One obeys the universal Spirit
   in order to evolve higher.*

8. Divine One of Trustworthiness (Figure 71)

(Figure 71)

*Following what is right
    is like a stream flowing toward the ocean.
Keeping one's innate virtue
    is the true foundation of happiness.
Through practicing great virtue,
    one can change one's personality
    and alter one's life.*

9. Divine One of Universal Mastery (Not pictured)
Raise left hand to duplicate the posture of the right hand in Figure 71, with wrists crossed.

*If you remove all covers and obstacles
    right here and now,
    you will know the origin of your life.
A long pilgrimage is not necessary
    to find your source.*

10. Divine One of Undefeatable Plainness (Figure 72)

*The road to becoming a Shien
    is clearly marked.*

100 Attune Your Body with Dao-In

*It is your impatience and desires
that blind your spiritual eyes.*

(Figure 72)

11. Divine One of Non-Aggression (Figure 73)

(Figure 73)

*Self-discipline alone
    will correctly develop your divine nature.
The subtle body,
    which will manifest itself,
    is the basis of your immortality.*

12. Divine One of Unconditional Supportiveness (Not pictured) Same as Figure 74 except right hand is open and palm up.

The subtle power
  comes not just from within ourselves,
  but is added
  as heaven, earth and all living things
  work positively through us.

13. Divine One of Pervasive Harmony (Not pictured) Same as Figure 74 except right thumb and index finger are touching tip to tip. Other fingers are held naturally.

Allow Tao to penetrate
  and it will expand,
  filling your body and being.
Your way of life will be
  naturally smooth and straight.
Wholehearted, and with
  strong protective power,
  you will forsake the bitterness of life,
  and be content within yourself.

14. Divine One of Subtle Universal Law (Figure 74)
Close right thumb inside of right fist.

(Figure 74)

*If you can adhere to the sacred method,
cultivating yourself precisely,
keeping clear as to
your every thought and motive,
then all good, positive qualities
will become firm
and all traps can be avoided.*

*You then become one with Tao,
unchanged even in death
as you realize the eternal firmness
of existence.*

15. Divine One of Subtle Light (Figure 75)

(Figure 75)

*The luminosity of pure mind
comes only with the death of desire.
As the mind dies, the spirit comes alive,
realizing an unusual majestic light.*

16. Divine One of Total Integration (Figure 76)
Left thumb and forefinger are touching tip to tip.
Other fingers held naturally.

*Persevere in connecting with
the universal light.*

*Through it you will achieve
    the fullness and brightness
    within your own nature.
You can experience and verify
    the greatness of eternal truth for yourself,
    and thereby voyage safely
    across the boundless spiritual ocean.*

(Figure 76)

17. **Divine One of Life-Giving Vitalization** (Not pictured) Same as Figure 76 except left thumb is closed inside left fist.

    *Never tire of studying life,
    Ceaselessly gather your chi and keep it whole.
    Essence, chi and spirit
        are the three jewels of life.*

18. **Divine One of Unaffected Clarity** (Figure 77) Thumb and index finger of both hands are touching tip to tip. Other fingers held naturally.

    *Unstain and empty the mind;
        thus it will become a fine tool
        that will unite the scattered fragments
        of yourself into one whole,
        so that What Is may become clear.*

104 Attune Your Body with Dao-In

(Figure 77)

19. Divine One of Great Silent Eloquence (Not Pictured) Arms crossed, right over left, over chest as in Figure 73 except thumb and index finger of both hands are touching tip to tip. Other fingers held naturally.

Tao is without color or form,
   yet from it emerges
   all wonders of the universe.
So subtly flows the Tao,
   deep within the fertile stillness,
   hushed within profound quietude.
It is indeed the Great Reality.

(Figure 78)

20. Divine One of Highest Awareness (Figure 78) Index finger and middle finger of left hand interlaced with index finger and middle finger of right hand.

Trace back to the root of your soul,
  found deep within your quiet reflections,
  and the ultimate truth unfolds naturally.

21. Divine One of Honest Nature (Figure 79)
Thumbs point upward with thumbprints touching. Fingers of both hands back to back and pointing to lower *tan tien* (but not too low, just below navel).

(Figure 79)

I keep my spirit untouched,
  my mind clear and detached,
  my body still and upright.
All my actions have a deep respect
  for the original stillness of the universe.
Though peacefully engaged in life,
  I abide in the infinite simplicity of Tao.

(Poetry excerpts are from *The Book of Changes and the Unchanging Truth*).

Note: After holding the arms in these postures, the following is beneficial: Sit crosslegged, extend arms so that hands are over each thigh, palms down and fingers of each hand pointing toward each other. Tip of left thumb touches tip of left index finger. Tip of right thumb touches tip of right index finger.

1. Bend wrist back straightening elbows fully.
2. Relax, allowing elbows to bend slightly.
3. Repeat steps 1 and 2 for a total of 21 times.

● This will release accumulated energy after meditation and help restore normalcy.

CONCLUDING SECTION

This section should be only done in the morning or early daytime. Avoid doing it in the evening or night. In the notes of different movements, I point out which ones are suitable for either day or night. For "night owls" who do not sleep at night or have different working hours, then these instructions are not relevant. They can try their own schedule or energy cycle in order to help themselves.

Certain *Dao-In* movements are suitable for nighttime; however, they do not include the ones in this set. In general, *Dao-In* exercise produces good health and longevity when done properly.

#50 Immortal Warming Up the Eyes

Beginning Posture: Sit crosslegged.

1. Rub the palms together until warm.

2. Place warm palms over eyes, pressing lightly (Figure 80).

(Figure 80)

3. Repeat steps 1 and 2 for a total of 3 times.

Note: Sit with spine straight.

#51 **Immortal Practicing Temple Acupressure**

Beginning Posture: Sit crosslegged.

1. With the back of the thumbs, rub the outside corner of both eyes in a circular motion 36 times (Figure 81).

(Figure 81)

Note: If the thumbs are not warm, rub the back of the thumbs on clothing before touching face.
● If there are sensitive points in this area, pressing them may work out tension.

#52 **Immortal Massaging the Nose**

Beginning Posture: Sit crosslegged.

1. Place the tips of the middle fingers on top of the index fingernails.

2. With hands in this position, rub the sides of the nose 36 times in a circular motion (Figure 82).

(Figure 82)

Note: Warm fingers first if cold.

#53 **Immortal Doing Eye Acupressure**

Beginning Posture: Sit crosslegged.

1. Place the tip of the middle fingers on top of the index fingernails.

2. Press the 3 points on the eyebrows and hold 5 seconds each
   a. Inside edge of eyebrow
   b. Middle of eyebrow
   c. Outer corner of eyebrow

3. Repeat step 2 for a total of 3 times.

Note: Press each day to relieve tension.

#54 Immortal Relaxing Neck Muscles

Beginning Posture: Sit crosslegged.

1. Rub the back of the neck and head with the left palm, 36 times.

2. Rub the back of the neck and head with the right palm, 36 times (Figure 83).

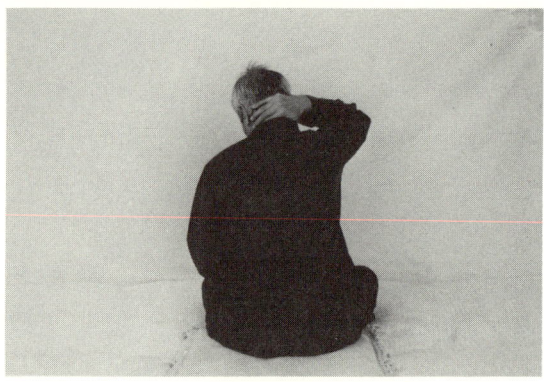

(Figure 83)

#55 Immortal Sharpening the Hearing

Beginning Posture: Sit crosslegged.

1. Rub over both ears with the palms, 36 times.

2. Press the palms firmly over both ears creating a tight seal (Figure 84).

3. Pull hands quickly straight out from the ears.

4. Repeat steps 2 and 3 for a total of 3 times.

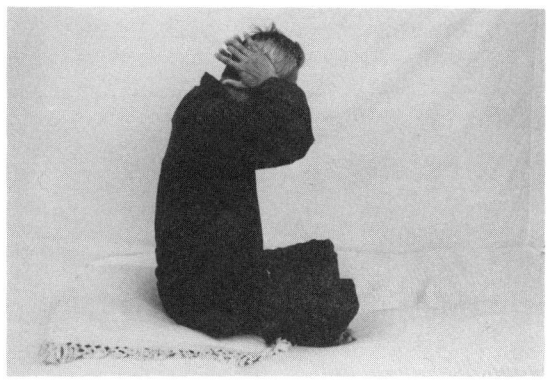

(Figure 84)

#56 Immortal Experiencing Gentle Rainfall

Beginning Posture: Sit crosslegged.

1. With the tips of all the fingers and thumbs, gently tap the head all over, stimulating the scalp for about one minute (Figure 85).

(Figure 85)

2. Massage the scalp with both hands, moving the scalp gently, then more vigorously, to stimulate it thoroughly.

3. With the palm side of the straight fingers of the right hand, gently tap all over the scalp 36 times.

112 *Attune Your Body with Dao-In*

4. With the palm side of the straight fingers of the left hand, gently tap all over the scalp 36 times.

#57 <u>**Immortal Imitating a Woodpecker**</u>

Beginning Posture: Sit crosslegged.

1. With the side of the right hand, strike the back of the neck up to the base of the skull 21 times.

2. With the side of the left hand, strike the back of the neck up to the base of the skull, 21 times (Figure 86).

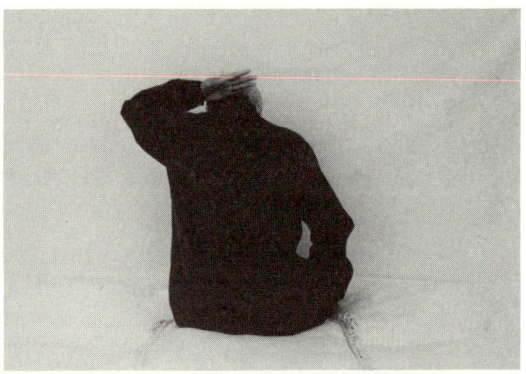

(Figure 86)

Note: This will release tension in the neck muscles and bring relaxation.

#58 <u>**Immortal Letting Go**</u>

Beginning Posture: Sit crosslegged.

1. Rub the scalp with the palms 36 times, alternating hands and moving from front to back.

#59 **Lying Meditation**

Beginning Posture: Lie on back, feet slightly apart and arms naturally alongside the body, palms up.

1. Breathe deeply and evenly, meditating for 3 minutes.

OPTIONAL SECTION

#60 Immortal Strengthening His Abdomen: For weak stomach or digestive problems

Beginning Posture: Lie on back with knees bent and feet flat on floor. Arms naturally alongside the body.

1. Cross right leg over left thigh

2. Straighten right leg.

3. With both hands massage the torso in large circles from the chest to lower abdomen.

4. Breathe deeply and rub for 5 minutes.

#61 Immortal Guarding His Energy: To prevent leak in sexual energy

1. Close the right nostril with second finger of left hand.

2. With the second finger of the right hand, press the perineum.

3. Inhale heavily, then exhale gently.

Note: Nocturnal emissions, or sexual leaks, may occur when asleep. If you notice energy building up in the sexual organs, immediately practice this exercise. Usually, after 6 breaths, the problem can be avoided.

● It is best to sleep on the left or right side of the body. Even if this practice does not stop the leak, it will rearrange your energy and make you feel better.

#62 Immortal's Breath Taming Active Energy: To prevent leak in sexual energy

Beginning Posture: Lie on right side with right hand on top of pillow, palm behind right ear (you may also place right hand between 2 pillows, palm up and rest head on pillow). Right leg straight, left leg bent at knee.

1. With left hand in a lightly clenched fist, press the area around navel and the area between the sexual organs and the navel while breathing in this manner. Inhale; hold breath for a short time and release.

2. Breathe 24 times.

Note: This exercise can help prevent sexual dreams or stop ejaculation.

#63 Immortal Strengthening Vital Energy: For extreme sexual weakness or for older or aged people.

Beginning Posture: Lie on your side.

1. Rub both hands together until they become very hot.

2. (Men) Hold over sexual organ or testicles. (Women) Place hands over sex organs.

3. Repeat 24 times.

#64 Immortal Strengthening Self: For general weakness, sexual weakness, or weakness due to excessive sex.

Beginning Posture: Lie on right side with right hand on top of pillow palm behind right ear. Left leg straight, right leg bent at knee.

1. Press the lower abdomen with left fist while breathing in this manner: concentrate on breathing through the tightened breathing tunnel, lengthening the inhale and controlling the exhale.

2. Repeat at least 36 times.

Note: This can help bring about a fast recovery. Even though you know how to recover fast, do not destroy your good energy again.

Afterword

Advice from Master Ni

You should learn *Dao-In* from my book or video, or from a certified Mentor registered with the College of Tao. There are many details in the deep sphere of *Dao-In* that you only learn by doing it year after year. In the beginning, choose what you can do, but keep the others in mind as a table of contents for future movement. Some movements are a little more difficult than others, and you can add those later. If you feel clumsy when you are doing it, do not worry; because you are doing it for yourself, not for show. Looking good is not required. Moving your energy and paying attention to what is happening inside your body is required. The goal of these movements is to benefit your life in a practical way.

A good time to do *Dao-In* is in the morning after rising. That depends, of course, on your personal schedule. Ancient people woke around 4:00 to start their day. Because they awoke so early, they did not have trouble finding enough time to do all kinds of different spiritual practices.

One principle I wish you would remember is that if you start to do it, you should follow the general sequence. Once you know the sequence, you can adjust it to suit your own needs. For example, you can switch the Preliminary Section and Closing Section. Especially in the morning, when your energy is in the process of waking up and growing stronger and stronger. At that time of day, it is suitable first to work on your face, and head. Then start to do the main section of *Dao-In*. After the main section, if you still have the time and interest, then do the Preliminary Section at the end.

Once you start, it is better keep the same schedule each day. For example, if you do it at 6 a.m., do it every day at that time. It is not wise to do it one day, skip several days, and then come back to it again. However, if you do it each day, some movements can be temporarily dropped. For example, if you find that some of the movements are very strenuous to one of your limbs or back, then do it one day and skip it for two days. You will not be missing anything by leaving a few movements out.

It is wise to adopt *Dao-In* as one of your life activities. Always remember that in doing any movement, the purpose of your practice is to develop a balance between your physical foundation and your spiritual potential.

Dao-In is fundamental. The movements of any style of *chi gong* practice can all be considered offspring of *Dao-In*. What I have given you in this book is like the trunk of a tree with many branches. This exercise was used by generations of immortals. If you do not have any other opportunity to learn other arts and knowledge from the tradition of Tao, do not feel insufficient or cheated by your circumstances. You are doing well by learning the main practice. Although development comes through many important experiences, if you only get a chance to learn *Dao-In* and you keep doing it, you will make some real progress and achieve direct spiritual inspiration. That is very possible. This is a framework of instruction I am providing for your spiritual development.

About Hua-Ching Ni

The author, Hua-Ching Ni, feels that it is his responsibility to ensure that people receive his message clearly and correctly, thus, he puts the lectures and classes in book form from various occasions with the single purpose of universal spiritual unity.

It will be his great happiness to see the genuine progress of all people, all societies and nations as one big harmonious worldly community. This is the goal that makes him talk and write as one way of fulfilling his personal duty.

What he offers people comes from his own growth and attainment. He began his personal spiritual pursuit when he was ten years old. Although his spiritual nature is innate, expressing it suitably and usefully requires world experience and learning.

When he is asked to give personal information, he says that there is personally nothing useful or worthy of mention. He feels that, as an individual, he is just one person living on the same plane of life with the rest of humanity and therefore he is not special. A hard life and hard work have made him deeper and stronger, and perhaps wiser. This is the case with all people who do not yield to the negative influences of life and the world. He does not work to establish himself as a special individual as people in general spiritual society do.

He likes to be considered a friend rather than be formally titled because he enjoys the natural spiritual response between himself and others who come together to extend the ageless natural spiritual truth to all.

He has been a great traveller. He has been in many places, and he never tires of going to new places. His books have been printed in different languages as a supplement to his professional work as a natural healer - a fully trained Traditional Chinese Medical doctor. He understands that his world mission is to awaken many people, and his friends and helpers as Mentors conjointly fulfill the world spiritual mission of this time.

Spiritual Study and Teaching Through the College of Tao

The College of Tao and the Union of Tao and Man were formally established in California in the 1970's, yet this tradition is a very old spiritual culture containing centuries of human spiritual growth. Its central goal is to offer healthy spiritual education to all people. This time-tested school values the spiritual development of each individual self and passes down its guidance and experience.

The College of Tao is a school which has no walls. The big human society is its classroom. Your own teaching and service is the class you attend; thus students grow from their lives and from studying the guidance of the Integral Way. The goal of the school is to help individuals develop themselves and become Mentors of the Integral Way. A Mentor is any individual who is spiritually self-responsible and who sets up the model of a healthy and complete life for oneself and others.

Any interested individual is welcome to join and learn to grow for oneself. The Correspondence Course/Self-Study Program can be useful to you. The Program, which is based on Master Ni's books and videotapes, gives people who wish to study on their own or are too far from a center or volunteer teachers an opportunity to study the learning of the Way at their own speed. The outline of how to participate in the Correspondence Course/Self-Study Program can be found at the end of the book *The Golden Message*.

It is recommended that all Mentors of the Integral Way use the self-study program in the *Golden Message* to educate themselves. They can teach special skills which are certified by the College of Tao. Those who engage in teaching with Master Ni's materials must follow the Mentor Service Regulations of the College of Tao. To receive recognition from the College of Tao for teaching activity, a Mentor must register with the College.

Mail to: College of Tao, 1314 Second Street, Santa Monica, CA 90401

_____ I wish to be put on the mailing list of the College of Tao and SevenStar Communications to be notified of educational activities and new publications.

_____ I wish to receive a list of Mentors teaching in my area or country.

_____ I am interested in the Correspondence Course/Self Study Program of the College of Tao. I have already read and understood the instruction for the Program printed in *The Golden Message*.

_____ I am interested in becoming a Mentor of the College of Tao.

Name:_____

Address:_____

City:_____State:_____Zip:_____

BOOKS IN ENGLISH BY HUA-CHING NI

Strength From Movement: Cultivating Chi - *New Publication!* by Hua-Ching Ni, Daoshing Ni and Maoshing Ni. *Chi,* the vital power of life, can be developed and cultivated within yourself to help support your health and your happy life. This book gives the deep reality of different useful forms of *chi* exercise and why certain types are more beneficial for certain types of people. Included are samples of several popular exercises. 256 pages, Softcover with 42 photographs, Stock No. BSTRE, $16.95.

The Time Is Now for a Better Life and a Better World
The purpose of achievement is on one hand to serve individual self-preservation and also to exercise one's attainment from spiritual cultivation to help all others. It is expected to save the difficulties of the time, to prepare ourselves to create a bright future for the human race and to overcome our modern-day spiritual dilemma by conjoint effort. 136 pages, Softcover, Stock No. BTIME, $10.95

The Way, the Truth and the Light
This is the story of the first sage who introduced the way to the world. The life of this young sage links the spiritual achievement of East and West and demonstrates the great spiritual virtue of his love to all people. 232 pages, Softcover, Stock No. BLIGH, $14.95

Life and Teaching of Two Immortals, Volume 2: Chen Tuan
The second emperor of the Sung Dynasty entitled Master Chen Tuan "Master of Supernatural Truth." Master Ni describes his life and cultivation and gives in-depth commentaries which provide teaching and insight into the achievement of this highly respected Master. 192 pages, Softcover, Stock No. BLIF2, $12.95

Esoteric Tao Teh Ching
Tao Teh Ching expresses the highest efficiency of life and can be applied in many levels of worldly life and spiritual life. This previously unreleased edition discusses instruction for spiritual practices in every day life, which includes important in-depth techniques for spiritual benefit. 192 pages, Softcover, Stock No. BESOT, $12.95

Golden Message - A Guide to Spiritual Life with Self-Study Program for Learning the Integral Way
This volume begins with a traditional treatise by Daoshing and Maoshing Ni about the broad nature of spiritual learning and its application for human life. It is followed by a message from Hua-Ching Ni. An outline of the Spiritual Self-Study Program and Correspondence Course of the College of Tao is included. 160 pages, Softcover, Stock No. BGOLD, $11.95

Internal Alchemy: The Natural Way to Immortality
Ancient spiritually achieved ones used alchemical terminology metaphorically for human internal energy transformation. Internal alchemy intends for an individual to transform one's emotion and lower energy to be higher energy and to find the unity of life in order to reach the divine immortality. 288 pages, Softcover, Stock No. BALCH, $15.95

Mysticism: Empowering the Spirit Within
For more than 8,000 years, mystical knowledge has been passed down by sages. Master Hua-Ching Ni introduces spiritual knowledge of the developed ones which does not use the senses or machines like scientific knowledge, yet can know both the entirety of the universe and the spirits. 200 pages, Softcover, Stock No. BMYST2, $13.95

Life and Teaching of Two Immortals, Volume 1: Kou Hong
Master Kou Hong was an achieved Master, a healer in Traditional Chinese Medicine and a specialist in the art of refining medicines who was born in 363 A.D. He laid the foundation of later cultural development in China. 176 pages, Softcover, Stock No. BLIF1, $12.95.

Ageless Counsel for Modern Life
These sixty-four writings, originally illustrative commentaries on the *I Ching*, are meaningful and useful spiritual guidance on various topics to enrich your life. Hua Ching Ni's delightful poetry and some teachings of esoteric Taoism can be found here as well. 256 pages, Softcover, Stock No. BAGEL, $15.95.

The Mystical Universal Mother
An understanding of both masculine and feminine energies are crucial to understanding oneself, in particular for people moving to higher spiritual evolution. Master Hua-Ching Ni focuses upon the feminine through the examples of some ancient and modern women. 240 pages, Softcover, Stock No. BMYST, $14.95

Moonlight in the Dark Night
To attain inner clarity and freedom of the soul, you have to control your emotions. This book contains wisdom on balancing the emotions, including balancing love relationships, so that spiritual achievement becomes possible. 168 pages, Softcover, Stock No. BMOON, $12.95

Harmony - The Art of Life
Harmony occurs when two different things find the point at which they can link together. Master Ni shares valuable spiritual understanding and insight about the ability to bring harmony within one's own self, one's relationships and the world. 208 pages, Softcover, Stock No. BHARM, $14.95

Attune Your Body with Dao-In
The ancients discovered that Dao-In exercises solved problems of stagnant energy, increased their health and lengthened their years. The exercises are also used as practical support for cultivation and higher achievements of spiritual immortality. 144 pages, Softcover with photographs, Stock No. BDAOI, $14.95 Also on VHS, Stock No. VDAOI, $39.95

The Key to Good Fortune: Refining Your Spirit
Straighten Your Way *(Tai Shan Kan Yin Pien)* and The Silent Way of Blessing *(Yin Chia Wen)* are the main guidance for a mature, healthy life. Spiritual improvement can be an integral part of realizing a Heavenly life on earth. 144 pages, Softcover, Stock No. BKEYT, $12.95

Eternal Light
Master Hua-Ching Ni presents the life and teachings of his father, Grandmaster Ni, Yo San, who was a spiritually achieved person, healer and teacher, and a source of inspiration to

Master Ni. Some deeper teachings and insights on living a spiritual life and higher achievement are given. 208 pages, Softcover, Stock No. BETER, $14.95

Quest of Soul
Hua-Ching Ni addresses many concepts about the soul such as saving the soul, improving the soul's quality, the free soul, what happens at death and the universal soul. He guides and inspires the reader into deeper self-knowledge and to move forward to increase personal happiness and spiritual depth. 152 pages, Softcover, Stock No. BQUES, $11.95

Nurture Your Spirits
Master Ni breaks some spiritual prohibitions and presents the spiritual truth he has studied and proven. This truth may help you develop and nurture your own spirits which are the truthful internal foundation of your life being. 176 pages, Softcover, Stock No. BNURT, $12.95

Internal Growth through Tao
Hua-Ching Ni teaches the more subtle, much deeper sphere of the reality of life that is above the shallow sphere of external achievement. He also clears the confusion caused by some spiritual teachings and guides you in the direction of developing spiritually by growing internally. 208 pages, Softcover, Stock No. BINTE, $13.95

Power of Natural Healing
Master Hua-Ching Ni discusses the natural capability of self-healing, information and practices which can assist any treatment method and presents methods of cultivation which promote a healthy life, longevity and spiritual achievement. 230 pages, Softcover, Stock No. BHEAL, $14.95

Essence of Universal Spirituality
In this volume, as an open-minded learner and achieved teacher of universal spirituality, Hua-Ching Ni examines and discusses all levels and topics of religious and spiritual teaching to help you understand the ultimate truth and enjoy the achievement of all religions without becoming confused by them. 304 pages, Softcover, Stock No. BESSE, $19.95

Guide to Inner Light
Drawing inspiration from the experience of the ancient achieved ones, modern people looking for the true source and meaning of life can find great teachings to direct and benefit them. The invaluable ancient development can teach us to reach the attainable spiritual truth and point the way to the Inner Light. 192 pages, Softcover, Stock No. BGUID, $12.95

Stepping Stones for Spiritual Success
In this volume, Master Ni has taken the best of the traditional teachings and put them into contemporary language to make them more relevant to our time, culture and lives. 160 pages, Softcover, Stock No. BSTEP, $12.95.

The Complete Works of Lao Tzu
The *Tao Teh Ching* is one of the most widely translated and cherished works of literature. Its timeless wisdom provides a bridge to the subtle spiritual truth and aids harmonious and peaceful living. Also included is the *Hua Hu Ching*, a later work of Lao Tzu which was lost to the general public for a thousand years. 212 pages, Softcover, Stock No. BCOMP, $12.95

The Book of Changes and the Unchanging Truth
The legendary classic *I Ching* is recognized as the first written book of wisdom. Leaders and sages throughout history have consulted it as a trusted advisor which reveals the appropriate action in any circumstance. Includes over 200 pages of background material on natural energy cycles, instruction and commentaries. 669 pages, Stock No. BBOOK, Hardcover, $35.00

The Story of Two Kingdoms
This volume is the metaphoric tale of the conflict between the Kingdoms of Light and Darkness. Through this unique story, Master Ni transmits esoteric teachings of Taoism which have been carefully guarded secrets for over 5,000 years. This book is for those who are serious in achieving high spiritual goals. 122 pages, Stock No. BSTOR, Hardcover, $14.50

The Way of Integral Life
This book includes practical and applicable suggestions for daily life, philosophical thought, esoteric insight and guidelines for those aspiring to serve the world. The ancient sages' achievement can assist the growth of your own wisdom and balanced, reasonable life. 320 pages, Softcover, Stock No. BWAYS, $14.00. Hardcover, Stock No. BWAYH, $20.00.

Enlightenment: Mother of Spiritual Independence
The inspiring story and teachings of Master Hui Neng, the father of Zen Buddhism and Sixth Patriarch of the Buddhist tradition, highlight this volume. Hui Neng was a person of ordinary birth, intellectually unsophisticated, who achieved himself to become a spiritual leader. 264 pages, Softcover, Stock No. BENLS, $12.50   Hardcover, Stock No. BENLH, $22.00.

Attaining Unlimited Life
Chuang Tzu was perhaps the greatest philosopher and master of Tao. He touches the organic nature of human life more deeply and directly than do other great teachers. This volume also includes questions by students and answers by Master Hua-Ching Ni. 467 pages, Softcover, Stock No. BATTS $18.00; Hardcover, Stock No. BATTH, $25.00.

The Gentle Path of Spiritual Progress
This book offers a glimpse into the dialogues between a master and his students. In a relaxed, open manner, Master Ni, Hua-Ching explains to his students the fundamental practices that are the keys to experiencing enlightenment in everyday life. 290 pages, Softcover, Stock No. BGENT, $12.95.

Spiritual Messages from a Buffalo Rider, A Man of Tao
Our buffalo nature rides on us, whereas an achieved person rides the buffalo. Hua-Ching Ni gives much helpful knowledge to those who are interested in improving their lives and deepening their cultivation so they too can develop beyond their mundane beings. 242 pages, Softcover, Stock No. BSPIR, $12.95.

8,000 Years of Wisdom, Volume I and II
This two-volume set contains a wealth of practical, down-to-earth advice given by Master Hua-Ching Ni over a five-year period. Drawing on his training in Traditional Chinese Medicine, Herbology and Acupuncture, Hua-Ching Ni gives candid answers to questions on many topics. Volume I includes dietary guidance; 236 pages; Stock No. BWIS1 Volume II includes sex and pregnancy guidance; 241 pages; Stock No. BWIS2. Softcover, each volume $12.50

Footsteps of the Mystical Child
This book poses and answers such questions as: What is a soul? What is wisdom? What is spiritual evolution? to enable readers to open themselves to new realms of understanding and personal growth. Includes true examples about people's internal and external struggles on the path of self-development and spiritual evolution. 166 pages, Softcover, Stock No. BFOOT, $9.50

The Heavenly Way
A translation of the classic Tai Shan Kan Yin Pien (Straighten Your Way) and Yin Chia Wen (The Silent Way of Blessing). The treatises in this booklet are the main guidance for a mature and healthy life. This truth can teach the perpetual Heavenly Way by which one reconnects oneself with the divine nature. 41 pages, Softcover, Stock No. BHEAV, $2.50

Workbook for Spiritual Development
This material summarizes thousands of years of traditional teachings and little-known practices for spiritual development. There are sections on ancient invocations, natural celibacy and postures for energy channeling. Master Ni explains basic attitudes and knowledge that supports spiritual practice. 240 pages, Softcover, Stock No. BWORK, $14.95

Poster of Master Lu
Color poster of Master Lu, Tung Ping (shown on cover of workbook), for use with the workbook or in one's shrine. 16" x 22"; Stock No. PMLTP. $10.95

The Taoist Inner View of the Universe
Master Hua-Ching Ni has given all the opportunity to know the vast achievement of the ancient unspoiled mind and its transpiercing vision. This book offers a glimpse of the inner world and immortal realm known to achieved ones and makes it understandable for students aspiring to a more complete life. 218 pages, Softcover, Stock No. BTAOI, $14.95

Tao, the Subtle Universal Law
Most people are unaware that their thoughts and behavior evoke responses from the invisible net of universal energy. To lead a good stable life is to be aware of the universal subtle law in every moment of our lives. This book presents practical methods that have been successfully used for centuries to accomplish this. 208 pages, Softcover, Stock No. BTAOS, $9.95

MATERIALS ON NATURAL HEALTH, ARTS AND SCIENCES

BOOKS

101 Vegetarian Delights by Lily Chuang and Cathy McNease
A vegetarian diet is a gentle way of life with both physical and spiritual benefits. The Oriental tradition provides helpful methods to assure that a vegetarian diet is well-balanced and nourishing. This book provides a variety of clear and precise recipes ranging from everyday nutrition to exotic and delicious feasts. 176 pages, Softcover, Stock No. B101V, $12.95

The Tao of Nutrition by Maoshing Ni, Ph.D., with Cathy McNease, B.S., M.H. - This book offers both a healing and a disease prevention system through eating habits. This volume contains 3 major sections: theories of Chinese nutrition and philosophy; descriptions of 100 common foods with energetic properties and therapeutic actions; and nutritional remedies for common ailments. 214 pages, Softcover, Stock No. BNUTR, $14.50

Chinese Vegetarian Delights by Lily Chuang
An extraordinary collection of recipes based on principles of traditional Chinese nutrition. For those who require restricted diets or who choose an optimal diet, this cookbook is a rare treasure. Meat, sugar, diary products and fried foods are excluded. 104 pages, Softcover, Stock No. BCHIV, $7.50

Chinese Herbology Made Easy - by Maoshing Ni, Ph.D.
This text provides an overview of Oriental medical theory, in-depth descriptions of each herb category, over 300 black and white photographs, extensive tables of individual herbs for easy reference and an index of pharmaceutical and Pin-Yin names. This book gives a clear, efficient focus to Chinese herbology. 202 pages, Softcover, Stock No. BCHIH, 14.50

Crane Style Chi Gong Book - By Daoshing Ni, Ph.D.
Chi Gong is a set of meditative exercises developed thousands of years ago in China and now practiced for healing purposes. It combines breathing techniques, body movements and mental imagery to guide the smooth flow of energy throughout the body. It may be used with or without the videotape. 55 pages. Stock No. BCRAN. Spiral-bound, $10.95

VIDEO TAPES

Attune Your Body with Dao-In (VHS) - by Master Hua-Ching Ni. Dao-In is a series of movements traditionally used for conducting physical energy. The ancients discovered that Dao-In exercise solves problems of stagnant energy, increases health and lengthens one's years, providing support for cultivation and higher achievements of spiritual immortality. Stock No. VDAOI, VHS $39.95

T'ai Chi Ch'uan: An Appreciation (VHS) - by Hua-Ching Ni.
Master Ni presents three styles of T'ai Chi handed down to him through generations of highly developed masters. "Gentle Path," "Sky Journey" and "Infinite Expansion" are presented uninterrupted in this unique videotape, set to music for observation and appreciation. Stock No. VAPPR. VHS 30 minutes $24.95

Crane Style Chi Gong (VHS) - by Dr. Daoshing Ni, Ph.D.
Chi Gong is a set of meditative exercises practiced for healing chronic diseases, strengthening the body and spiritual enlightenment. Correct and persistent practice will increase one's energy, relieve tension, improve concentration, release emotional stress and restore general well-being. 2 hours, Stock No. VCRAN. $39.95

Eight Treasures (VHS) - By Maoshing Ni, Ph.D.
These exercises help open blocks in your energy flow and strengthen your vitality. It is a complete exercise combining physical stretching, toning and energy-conducting movements coordinated with breathing. Patterned from nature, its 32 movements are an excellent foundation for T'ai Chi Ch'uan or martial arts. 1 hour, 45 minutes. Stock No. VEIGH. $39.95

T'ai Chi Ch'uan I & II (VHS) - By Maoshing Ni, Ph.D.
This exercise integrates the flow of physical movement with that of internal energy in the Taoist style of "Harmony," similar to the long form of Yang-style T'ai Chi Ch'uan. T'ai Chi has been practiced for thousands of years to help both physical longevity and spiritual cultivation. 1 hour each. Each videotape $39.95. Order both for $69.95. Stock Nos: Part I, VTAI1; Part II, VTAI2; Set of two, VTAI3.

AUDIO CASSETTES

Colored Dust
This graceful, sensitive tribute by singer-songwriter Gaillee to the inner being that transcends everyday mediocrity combines a rich palette of colorful music with the moving poetry of Master Ni, Hua-Ching. Cassette Stock No. ADUST $10.98, CD Stock No. ADUST2 $15.98.

Invocations for Health, Longevity and Healing a Broken Heart - By Maoshing Ni, Ph.D.
This audio cassette guides the listener through a series of ancient invocations to channel and conduct one's own healing energy and vital force. "Thinking is louder than thunder. The mystical power which creates all miracles is your sincere practice of this principle." 30 minutes, Stock No. AINVO, $9.95

Stress Release with Chi Gong - By Maoshing Ni, Ph.D.
This audio cassette guides you through simple, ancient breathing exercises that enable you to release day-to-day stress and tension that are such a common cause of illness today. 30 minutes. Stock No. ACHIS. $9.95

Pain Management with Chi Gong - By Maoshing Ni, Ph.D.
Using easy visualization and deep-breathing techniques developed over thousands of years, this audio cassette offers methods for overcoming pain by invigorating your energy flow and unblocking obstructions that cause pain. 30 minutes, Stock No. ACHIP. $9.95

***Tao Teh Ching* Cassette Tapes**
This classic work of Lao Tzu has been recorded in this two-cassette set that is a companion to the book translated by Hua-Ching Ni. Professionally recorded and read by Robert Rudelson. 120 minutes. Stock No. ATAOT. $12.95

How To Order

Name: _____

Address: _____

City: _____ State: _____ Zip: _____

Phone - Daytime: _____ Evening: _____

(We may telephone you if we have questions about your order.)

Qty.	Stock No.	Title/Description	Price Each	Total Price

Total amount for items ordered_____

Sales tax (CA residents only, 8-1/4%)_____

Shipping Charge (see below)_____

Total Amount Enclosed_____

Visa _____ Mastercard _____ Expiration Date _____

Card number:_____

Signature:_____

Prices subject to change without notice.

Shipping: Please give full street address or nearest crossroads. If shipping to more than one address, use separate shipping charges. Please allow 2 - 4 weeks for US delivery and 6 - 10 weeks for foreign surface mail.

By Mail: Complete this form with payment (US funds only, No Foreign Postal Money Orders, please) and mail to: SevenStar Publications, 1314 Second St., Santa Monica, CA 90401.

Phone Orders: You may leave credit card orders anytime on our answering machine. Please speak clearly and remember to leave your full name and daytime phone number. Call (800) 578-9526 to order or (310) 576-1901 for information..

<u>Shipping Charges:</u>

Domestic Surface: First item $3.25, each additional, add $.50.
Canada Surface: First item $3.25, each additional, add $1.00.
Canada Air: First item $4.00, each additional, add $2.00.
Foreign Surface: First item $3.50, each additional, add $2.00.
Foreign Air: First item $12.00, each additional, add $7.00.

<u>All foreign orders:</u> Add 5% of your book total to shipping charges to cover insurance.

_____ Please send me your complete catalog.

Thank you for your order.

Yo San University of Traditional Chinese Medicine
"Not just a medical career, but a life-time commitment to raising one's spiritual standard."

Thank you for your support and interest in our publications and services. It is by your patronage that we continue to offer you the practical knowledge and wisdom from this venerable Taoist tradition.

Because of your sustained interest in Taoism, in January 1989 we formed Yo San University of Traditional Chinese Medicine, a non-profit educational institution under the direction of founder Master Ni, Hua-Ching. Yo San University is the continuation of 38 generations of Ni family practitioners who handed down knowledge and wisdom from father to son. Its purpose is to train and graduate practitioners of the highest caliber in Traditional Chinese Medicine, which includes acupuncture, herbology and spiritual development.

We view Traditional Chinese Medicine as the application of spiritual development. Its foundation is the spiritual capability to know life, to diagnose a person's problem and how to cure it. We teach students how to care for themselves and others, emphasizing the integration of traditional knowledge and modern science. Yo San University offers a complete Master's degree program approved by the California State Department of Education that provides an excellent education in Traditional Chinese Medicine and meets all requirements for state licensure.

We invite you to inquire into our university for a creative and rewarding career as a holistic physician. Classes are also open to persons interested only in self-enrichment. For more information, please fill out the form below and send it to:

Yo San University
of Traditional Chinese Medicine
1314 Second Street
Santa Monica, CA 90401

☐ Please send me information on the Masters degree program in Traditional Chinese Medicine.

☐ Please send me information on health workshops and seminars.

☐ Please send me information on continuing education for acupuncturists and health professionals.

Name_____

Address_____

City_____State_____Zip_____

Phone(day)_____(evening)_____

Herbs Used by Ancient Masters

The pursuit of everlasting youth or immortality throughout human history is an innate human desire. Long ago, Chinese esoteric Taoists went to the high mountains to contemplate nature, strengthen their bodies, empower their minds and develop their spirit. From their studies and cultivation, they gave China alchemy and chemistry, herbology and acupuncture, the I Ching, astrology, martial arts and T'ai Chi Ch'uan, Chi Gong and many other useful kinds of knowledge.

Most important, they handed down in secrecy methods for attaining longevity and spiritual immortality. There were different levels of approach; one was to use a collection of food herb formulas that were only available to highly achieved Taoist masters. They used these food herbs to increase energy and heighten vitality. This treasured collection of herbal formulas remained within the Ni family for centuries.

Now, through Traditions of Tao, the Ni family makes these foods available for you to use to assist the foundation of your own positive development. It is only with a strong foundation that expected results are produced from diligent cultivation.

As a further benefit, in concert with the Taoist principle of self-sufficiency, Traditions of Tao offers the food herbs along with the Union of Tao and Man's publications in a distribution opportunity for anyone serious about financial independence.

Send to: Traditions of Tao
*   1314 Second Street #208*
*   Santa Monica, CA 90401*

Please send me a Traditions of Tao brochure.

Name_____

Address_____

City_____State_____Zip_____

Phone (day)_____(night)_____

Index of Some Topics

abdomen 31, 39, 51, 52, 55, 87, 88, 95, 114, 116
arms 9, 29-31, 37, 47-52, 55, 57, 67, 75, 78, 79, 81, 84, 85, 86, 91, 97, 98, 104, 105, 113-114
arthritis 2, 76
bladder 26
bones 2, 5, 9, 29, 94
breath 11, 51, 58, 71, 83, 91, 94, 115
chi 1, 10, 13, 23, 27, 29, 103, 118
Chuang Tzu 11
communism 16
day 10, 23, 24, 62, 67-69, 73-75, 78, 80, 94, 107, 109, 117-118
desire 2, 18, 19, 21, 102
digestive problems 114
dizziness 27
ears 7, 60, 61, 96, 110
eating 65
Eight Treasures 7
evening 23, 24, 29, 74, 80, 92, 107
eyebrows 109
eyes 7, 21, 96, 100, 107, 108
face 9, 10, 41, 54, 93, 97, 108, 117
feet 9, 30, 31, 37-40, 47, 48, 50, 90, 113, 114
fists 63, 78, 83, 84
government 16-19, 21
heart 94-96
immortality 2, 3, 7, 12, 27, 100
joints 2, 29
kidneys 54, 55, 74, 95
Lao Tzu 5, 6, 19
legs 29-31, 34-36, 41, 42, 44, 45, 47-52, 55, 57, 80, 81, 86, 89
longevity 2, 3, 27, 107
martial arts 27, 28
meditation 4, 7, 8, 10, 12, 13, 27, 63, 93-95, 106, 113
mental health 13
morning 23, 24, 26, 29, 58, 61, 62, 65, 74, 88, 91, 107, 117
muscles 9, 11, 28-30, 80, 110, 112
neck 9, 26, 38, 40, 80, 91, 110, 112
night 24, 29, 58, 60, 67-70, 74, 89-92, 94, 107
normalcy 9, 106
nose 45, 46, 73, 94, 108, 109
Pa Kun Dao-In 7
pain 29, 30
polarity pressure 57
Pong Tzu 6, 28
quiet sitting 13, 95
rheumatism 2, 76
scalp 92, 111, 112
self-cultivation 3, 4, 7, 8
sex 3, 6, 115
sexual energy 13, 27, 114, 115
sexual organs 114, 115
shoulders 30, 37, 38, 47, 49, 51, 52, 75
skull 57, 60, 61, 95, 112
sleep 17, 23, 24, 29, 91, 93, 107, 114
solar energy 23
spinal cord 29
spine 9, 28, 54, 55, 74, 94, 95, 108
stagnation 2, 8-10
stomach 29, 47, 59, 71, 78, 88, 114
subtle energy 6
t'ai chi 1, 10, 23, 29
tailbone 36, 49, 54, 55
tan tien 21, 74, 94, 105
Tao Teh Ching 5, 12
Taoist Canon 4
temples 62
tendons 9, 29
three key points 95
tongue 7, 73, 74
torso 36, 37, 41, 42, 47, 51-54, 72, 76, 114
Traditional Chinese Medicine 3, 5, 60
waist 58-63, 71, 75-78, 90
weight 49, 78
Wen Tzu 19
wind pond 60, 61
Yellow river 2
yin and *yang* 4, 9